The Dynamics of
Development
and
Development
Administration

Recent Titles in
Contributions in Economics and Economic History

The Dynamics of
Development
and
Development
Administration

KEMPE RONALD HOPE

CONTRIBUTIONS IN ECONOMICS AND
ECONOMIC HISTORY, NUMBER 56

GREENWOOD PRESS
Westport, Connecticut
London, England

Library of Congress Cataloging in Publication Data

CC,

Hope, Kempe R.
  The dynamics of development and development
administration.

  (Contributions in economics and economic history,
ISSN 0084-9235 ; no. 56)
  Includes bibliographical references and index.
  1. Economic development. 2. Developing countries—
Economic policy. 3. Public administration—
Developing countries. I. Title. II. Title: Develop-
ment administration. III. Series.
  HD82.H59   1984   351.82'09172'4   83-16623
  ISBN 0-313-24269-0 (lib. bdg.)

Library of Congress Catalog Card Number: 83-16623
ISBN: 0-313-24269-0
ISSN: 0084-9235

First published in 1984

Greenwood Press
A division of Congressional Information Service, Inc.
88 Post Road West
Westport, Connecticut 06881

Printed in the United States of America

10 9 8 7 6 5 4 3 2 1

To
Evadnie, Kempe, Jr., Euclyn
and
Jesse Burkhead—Teacher and Friend

Contents

Tables

Preface

What is meant by development? What is development administration? What is the necessary interaction between these two concepts to bring about socioeconomic change? Though the opinions may vary with respect to the meaning of these concepts, there is indeed a general consensus that development cannot occur without the proper development administration machinery.

This work analyses the evolutionary thought on the two concepts of "development" and "development administration" and interprets their dynamic nature with primary emphasis on their current perspectives and dimensions in an attempt to shed some light on the problems, policy approaches, and synthesis currently associated with their applications in developing nations.

In preparing this book I benefited from the valuable assistance of many individuals who are too numerous to mention. However, I must acknowledge the dedicated research and editorial assistance of Evadnie Hope as well as the consistent typing skills of my secretary Mrs. Sue Cleary. I would also like to mention Professor Jesse Burkhead, Dr. Aubrey Armstrong and Dr. Kemal Bas who provided me with valuable comments and suggestions on earlier drafts of the manuscript. Any errors or omissions, however, remain my sole responsibility.

The Dynamics of
Development
and
Development
Administration

1

Introduction

For more than two decades now, growing worldwide attention has been focused on the dynamics of development and development administration in developing nations. The United Nations has sponsored development decades; rich countries pay much lip service to development; and millions of poor people in several developing nations have set development as their most sought-after goal. Indeed, this is the first time in history that it has been possible to conceive of development for many of the countries in the world economy (Hunter, 1971:1).

But what is development and development administration? How is development recognised when it occurs? What are the problems associated with the administration of development in developing nations? From an examination of the voluminous literature on development there seems to be much disagreement on what development is all about and how it should be measured. There is, however, a fairly general consensus on the meaning and significance of development administration.

This work focuses on the dynamic nature of development and development administration in developing nations with primary emphasis on the current perspectives and dimensions of the two concepts and an analytical appraisal of the problems associated with applications of these concepts in developing nations.

The problems of economic development, confronted by two-thirds of the world's population, pose a formidable challenge to the decision makers in those countries. As such, politicians and development administrators in developing nations often find themselves baffled by the sheer magnitude and complexity of the issues, as well as the possible policy choices available to overcome some of the problems. This work is, therefore, intended to shed some light on these issues and the current policy approaches vis-à-vis the interaction between development and development administration.

During the process of development, the functions of government grow further not only in size, magnitude and importance but also in complexity. *Complexity* is used here to denote a high degree of knowledge required to produce the output of a system and a high degree of division of labour. Government activities become much more specialised, requiring highly technical personnei to handle them. They often involve more than one discipline and cut across traditional functions, requiring interdisciplinary and multifunctional approaches. They are also multidimensional in nature. They are influenced by a high degree of interdependence among individuals and groups. They also involve different levels of government, including central, regional and local administration and often cut across traditional geographical or political boundaries.

One aspect of the differentiation of functions has been the rise of the bureaucracy as a distinct arm of government. It is true that the arts of government and administration have been essential features of human society ever since man emerged from the most primitive form of association. But modern development administration has a very short history. A country can be said to have established a modern system of development administration only when it has a civil service to serve the country, the nation, the State or Head of State in his or her capacity as a symbol of the nation. In other words, modern development administration is one in which the administrators are not servants of any other person or group of persons, but servants of the public. Once the position as a public servant is established, a development administrator assumes a role distinct from that of a politician.

Development administration is a means to an end insofar as the means can be separated from the end. It is an instrument to implement public policy. It is a detailed and systematic execution of public law. Its operations are goal oriented and are for the purpose of fulfilling government policies. Administrative management of national development is a process of organising collective efforts to achieve particular objectives as determined by the economic and political system or, more simply, to get things done through national organisations (Hope, 1979b:2–3).

The concept of economic development has become very commonplace in this century and there is a growing body of literature on its historical development. Moreover, economists have gone to great lengths to differentiate between the terms *economic development* and *economic growth*. It is now recognised that they are two different, but related, processes that are both counterparts and competitors, depending on the time span involved, and that the distinction is important from both theoretical and policymaking standpoints (Flammang, 1979:47).

In the commonly used meanings of the two terms, they are clearly complementary processes, each having the potential of contributing to the success of the other. But this does not negate their competitive nature. Unusually favourable growing conditions may easily result in impressive growth for a country's traditional output or in increased leisure for its population, without much if any structural change, as was the case in Liberia (Clower et al., 1966). Similarly, development is possible without growth. One sector may grow at the expense of another. Industrial expansion may be matched by a decline in the agricultural sector, for example, as was the case in the Caribbean (Hope, 1981a).

The development-growth distinction is essential in economic thinking. Growth and development are different processes that are complementary in the long run but competitive in the short run. Economic growth is a process of simple increase, implying more of the same, while economic development is a process of structural change, implying something different if not something more (Flammang, 1979:50–61).

All through the interwar years, the term *economic development*, when it was used outside the Marxist literature, continued to denote the development or exploitation of natural resources. In the immediate postwar years, *economic development* became virtually synonymous with growth in per capita income in developing nations (Arndt, 1982:463–65). From the 1970s onward, disappointment over the lack of widespread socioeconomic advances, even under conditions of very rapid economic growth, led to the widespread adoption of an alternative conception of economic development. According to this new viewpoint, economic development should be regarded in terms of progress toward reducing the incidences of poverty, unemployment and income inequalities. For those whose living standards have not been increasing, the eradication of those conditions, and not rising per capita income, is clearly the essence of development (Zuvekas, 1979:11).

During the immediate postwar period to the present time, there have been several contrasting perceptions of development (Streeten, 1979b:25–27). In the 1940s the less affluent countries located in Africa, Asia and Latin America were usually described as backward. By the 1950s the term *backward*, with its pejorative connotations, had been generally discarded in favour of the term *underdeveloped*, which implies the existence of a potential that could be realised and does not suggest directly, at least, an attitude of superiority on the part of industrialised nations. In the 1960s, we began to refer to these countries as less developed, an even more acceptable term, since the countries in question are developed only less so than some others. Moreover, the expression "Third World countries" became prominent and was used to distinguish these nations from the Western industrialised nations, on the one hand, and the Eastern socialist nations, on the other. In the 1970s, several new terms came to be commonly used. One was the expression "developing nations," which seems to remove all implications of inferiority. A distinction has also been made between the "oil-producing" and "non-oil-producing nations" (Zuvekas, 1979:8–9). At the present time, the apellations "less-developed countries" (LDC's) and "developing nations" are the most widely used and are used interchangeably. In this work they will be so used.

Apart from the contrasting perceptions of development, there have also been many development fashions over the years (Haq, 1976:20). During the immediate postwar period, priority was given to import-substitution policies. Import-substituting industries became the key to development. In the early 1960s, import-substitution policies were discarded and rapid industrialisation for export expansion became the task. In the mid–1960s, rapid industrialisation was regarded as an illusion and rapid agricultural growth became the only road to development. In the latter part of the 1960s, the LDCs began to give priority to population control policies because of the general thinking that all development is likely to be submerged by the population explosion. From the 1970s onward the general thinking has been that the poor masses have not gained much from development. This has led to the rejection of policies in favour of growth in gross national product (GNP) and to the adoption of policies in favour of distribution and the provision of basic needs for the poor.

2

The Concept of Development

Despite the existence of a great body of literature on the concept of development there is still a great degree of ambiguity surrounding its meaning. Development has been defined in a number of ways incorporating various elements of the social, political, cultural and economic system. As such, despite some consensus of what constitutes underdevelopment there is no real agreement on what is meant by development. The concept of development, therefore, has been plagued with ever-changing definitions and policy applications to the extent that the methods advocated for achieving development have multiplied at a faster rate than they have been applied in some developing nations. Now, let us analyse the evolution of this concept in greater detail.

THE ECONOMIC DIMENSION

For many years, almost everyone looked at the development of poor countries solely in terms of economic goals. Development meant a rising gross national product, an increase in investment and consumption (the twin pillars of traditional economics) and a rising standard of living. A theory was elaborated on the basis of Western experience during the nineteenth century. According to that theory, at some point a developing economy would become strong enough, and complex enough, to take off toward the industrial heights scaled by so many countries in the Northern Hemisphere (Hope, 1979a:11). The tools of this type of development, also, were quite clearly anything that could help get the engines of investment, production and consumption moving in the individual poor country. This meant an inflow of capital goods from rich countries. It also meant technical advice, borne either by experts from abroad or by students returning home with degrees in economics from North American and European universities and the creation of economic institutions that would provide people in the less-developed countries with the ability to read and write and enable them to produce more economic and technical know-how.

Round and round the system would go, getting steadily richer, until the poor country could truly be said to be developing. This theory of economic development worked remarkably well in some countries. In South Korea and Taiwan, for example, production of goods and services leaped upward—helped, of course, by U.S. aid and defense outlays—until these countries began to leave poverty behind (Hunter, 1971:2).

The major emphasis of this type of development was on linearity. Development was regarded as a linear path along which all countries travelled. Development was seen primarily as economic growth, and it was taken for granted that organising the march along the development path was the prime concern of government. This model of development had a powerful grip on the imagination of policymakers in the industrialised nations despite its criticisms by many academics.

The linear view resulted in a number of questions about the nature, causes and objectives of development. It was criticised on logical, moral, political and historical grounds. Elsewhere, some other flaws appeared in the theory. For one thing, the poor countries challenged the notion that development could be measured purely in terms of growth in GNP. In country after country, it became obvious that there were serious questions to be asked about economic justice, social equality and political development, the nature and rate of change, the internal consistency of the development process and income distribution. Hence, the challenge resulted in a search for a new meaning and approach to development—a relative one. "The task was therefore one of finding a new measure of development to replace the growth or national income measure, or, more precisely, to enable the national income to be given its true, somewhat limited, significance as a measure of development potential" (Seers, 1969:3).

WHOLISTIC VIEW OF DEVELOPMENT

Many theorists and the leaders of the developing Third World countries, therefore, agreed on the principle that underdevelopment is not just the lack of development. They argued instead that before there was development there was no underdevelopment and that the relationship between development and underdevelopment is not just a comparative one, in the sense that some places are more developed or less developed than others, but, rather, that development and underdevelopment are related through the common historical process they have shared during the past several centuries and through the mutual (that is, reciprocal) influence they have had, still have and will continue to have, on each other throughout history (Frank, 1975:1; Seers, 1977:2–7). The emphasis therefore shifted, and development began to be regarded as a total process involving economic, social, political and cultural elements. Its principal aim being to improve not only the economic but the social, cultural and environmental welfare of a nation. This was to be brought about not through reliance on external assistance but through national effort embodied in local community participation and targeted at removing all signs of "external economic dependence."

This new definition of development stresses the importance of local considerations in the formulation of development policies and programs. Local needs and values would determine the direction development would take in a particular country, and local institutions would be responsible for carrying it out (Kasdan, 1973:10). Recent evaluations of development activities have both exemplified and influenced this emerging new approach to development (Lisk, 1977:175–91). Their similar diagnoses of the ills of the development system represent a much deeper understanding than did the one-sided explanations frequently offered in the postwar period for the failure of policies and programs—for example, a lack of infrastructure, industrialisation, education and modern agricultural policies.

Without a doubt, the new concept of development, particularly the emphasis on economic independence, has for the first time resulted in a significant shift in the balance of economic power in favour of some developing countries. This shift in the balance of economic power was initiated by the embargo action taken by the oil-exporting countries toward the end of 1973. This was followed by a rapidly growing awareness on the part of developing countries of the need for joint action to improve their bargaining position and to protect their economic interests (Hope, 1979a:13).

Essentially, the current thrust toward development can be viewed as a process in eradicating the state of economic dependence that was brought about when some nations became rich at the expense of others. The current policy of self-reliance implies the full utilisation of the domestic resources of developing countries by developing countries and close economic cooperation among them to achieve agreed-on objectives (Parmar, 1975). The final result is intended to be an end to external economic dependence, social and cultural deprivation, political subjugation, and environmental degradation and is further intended to bring about a redistribution of income. Hence, what is now required is an elaboration by the developing countries of this comprehensive strategy for strengthening their mutual cooperation in all aspects of their economic relations. Such an elaboration of the strategy should include, *inter alia*, measures designed specifically to promote the flows of trade and finance among developing countries; measures to encourage joint ventures involving the technology and know-how of developed nations (both market economy and socialist); and measures to build up an independent and viable scientific and technological base, to take the first step toward harmonising respective economic development programmes (Parmar, 1975:3–27).

Development in this context is seen as development of every man and woman—of the whole man and woman—and not just the growth of things, which are merely means. Development is geared to the satisfaction of needs, beginning with the needs of the poor who constitute the world's majority. At the same time, development is seen to ensure the humanisation of man by the satisfaction of man's needs for expression, creativity, conviviality and deciding man's own destiny. Development, therefore, is a whole. It is an integral, value-loaded, cultural process and it encompasses the natural, environmental and social relations—education, production, consumption and well-being. It is endogenous and springs from the heart of each society, which relies first on its own strength and resources and defines in sovereignty the vision of its future; cooperating with societies sharing its problems and aspirations. In general, the aim of development should be to achieve a more equitable distribution of the benefits of growth in the whole economy (Seers, 1977:5–6) and as such, must be thought of in terms of evolution rather than in terms of creation.

Development does not start with goods; it starts with people and their education, organisation and discipline (Schumacher, 1974:140–41). Without these three, all resources remain latent, untapped potential. Here, then, lies the central problem of development and the reason why development cannot be an act of creation or why it cannot be bought or accelerated through aid. It requires a process of evolution. If aid is given to introduce certain new economic activities, the activities will be beneficial and viable only if they can be sustained by the already existing educational level of fairly broad groups of people, and they will be truly valuable only if they promote and spread advances in education, organisation and discipline (Schumacher, 1974:140–41). It follows from this that development entails a direct internal attack that takes poverty seriously. It will not go on mechanically. It will concern itself with people because people represent the primary source and the ultimate beneficiaries of the development process. It means, at least, the provision of basic needs for the masses.

THE BASIC-NEEDS APPROACH

The primary objective of a basic-needs approach to development is to provide opportunities for the full physical, mental and social development of the individual (Streeten, 1979a:136). This approach focuses on mobilising particular resources for particular groups identified as deficient in these resources and concentrates on the nature of what is provided rather than on income. The basic-needs approach does not rely solely on income generation or transfers and places primary emphasis on the production and delivery to the intended groups of the basic-needs basket through supply management and a delivery system (Srinivasan, 1977:18).

The basic-needs approach differs conceptually from other poverty-oriented development strategies (Streeten and Burki, 1978:411–21). First, whereas conventional antipoverty programmes are directed at target poverty groups within an economy, the basic-needs approach is founded on the premise that poverty in most developing countries is widespread and that action should therefore be directed at the population as a whole. Second, the basic-needs approach is concerned with significantly raising the level of aggregate demand and with increasing the supply of basic goods and services as opposed to merely raising the incomes of the poor to a minimum subsistence level. Actually, basic-needs policies are not restricted to the eradication of absolute poverty but extend to the satisfaction of needs over and above the subsistence level as a means of eliminating relative poverty through a continuous process of economic development and social progress (Lisk, 1977:186). Another difference lies in the fact that the basic-needs approach stresses effective mass participation in both the formulation and implementation of policy measures as a way of ensuring that its main objective is not forgotten.

In defining the objectives and distinguishing features of a basic-needs policy approach, recognition must be given to the fact that countries will have different requirements because of differences in their economic, political, social and cultural characteristics. As a result, there are no objective criteria for defining the contents of a basic-needs bundle. While certain minimum physiological conditions are necessary to sustain life, basic needs vary between geographical areas, cultures and time periods. It makes little sense, therefore, to attempt to define universal standards of basic needs. Moreover, there is not a single level of basic needs but a hierarchy (Streeten and Burki, 1978:413). Given such a hierarchy, societies can define their own basket of basic goods and services which would, out of necessity, differ according to the society's objectives. However, the basic-needs approach sets priorities in production and distribution. It gives the first priority to the production of what is essential to meet human needs in such a way that it goes to meet the needs of the most needy. It gives a much lower priority to production of goods for other human needs, for non-basic needs and for the needs of the less needy.

The basic-needs approach does not call for asceticism or puritanism. All that it insists on is a certain order of priorities: first meet the basic needs of those most in need and then, *and only then*, go about satisfying other needs if they are felt. The basic theoretical and empirical question in connection with the basic-needs approach has to do with the ordering of these pursuits in terms of time. The assumption is that the pursuit of non-basic needs will stand in the way of meeting basic needs (Loup, 1983:127–38).

The autonomy of societies in deciding their own basket of basic goods is also consistent with the Declaration of Principles and Programme of Action of the World Employment Conference in 1976. In that conference, it was declared that it is important to recognise that the concept of basic needs is a country-specific and dynamic concept and that it should be placed within a context of a nation's overall economic and social development (ILO, 1977:24). It was further stated that basic needs "in no circumstances should be taken to mean merely the minimum necessary for subsistence; it should be placed within a context of national independence, the dignity of individuals and peoples and their freedom to chart their destiny without hindrance" (ILO, 1977:24).

The satisfaction of basic needs in developing countries cannot be achieved without both acceleration in their economic growth and measures aimed at changing the pattern of growth and access to the use of productive resources by the lowest income groups. The redistribution factor is also important here. To be of use this redistribution must result in the production of more basic goods and services. Moreover, the provision of adequate employment opportunities is an essential ingredient in this strategy. The productive mobilisation of the unemployed, the seasonally unemployed and the underemployed, plus higher productivity by the working poor, are essential means of ensuring both a level of output high enough to meet basic-needs targets and their proper distribution (ILO, 1976:43).

The basic-needs approach, however, cannot and should not be interpreted as an exclusive concern with the production of basic goods and the shift toward more labour-intensive methods. On the contrary, as well as expanding the production of basic goods using different levels of technology, it is necessary to make proper provision for adequate supplies of intermediate and capital goods (Kuzmin, 1977:338). The precise combination of these goods will have to be determined by the specific economic condition existing in each country, particularly the level of technology.

This raises an important issue in the provision of many of the basic needs—the question of transfer of appropriate technology. Technology has long been recognised as an important factor in development. Historical studies have demonstrated the substantial contribution of technological progress to the long-term rise in productivity of labour and output in the developed nations and its impact on the level and structure of employment and incomes. But the role of technology in less-developed nations has been subject to a great deal of controversy. Let us move on now to discuss the issue of technology transfer within the framework of basic-needs development in the Third World.

TECHNOLOGY TRANSFER FOR BASIC-NEEDS DEVELOPMENT

Technology can be defined as the skills, knowledge and procedures used in the provision of goods and services for any given society. Due to the unique features of each developing economy, technology must be discussed in the context of what is appropriate. But the concept of "appropriate technology" sometimes meets with the criticism that it carries a neocolonial connotation; a connotation that the existing, modern and efficient technology is unsuitable for the less-developed countries, which should be satisfied with something inferior that would result in and perpetuate a technological gap. But this is erroneous. The gap exists in the fact that some countries are poor while others are rich. The task is to reduce or eliminate this gap, which is an economic one (Singer, 1977:9). If the problem is regarded as a technological gap and similar technology is applied to the two groups of countries (developed and less developed), the real economic gap will increase rather than decline unless other measures are taken.

The concept of appropriate technology must be looked at only in relation to some specific historical context and in terms of demand (basic-needs goals) and supply (the appropriate production processes) (Ndongko and Anyang, 1981:35–43; Watanabe, 1980:167–84). There is an urgent need for a harmonisation of these two factors to bring about the management and production techniques that are best suited to the resources and future development potential of the individual developing countries (McRobie, 1979:71–86). Such technology must contribute to greater productive employment opportunities, elimination of poverty and the achievement of an equitable distribution of income.

Technological decisions and the pace of technical change affect all development processes and, in turn, are affected by them. The various combinations and proportions in which labour, material resources and capital are used influence not only the type and quantity of goods and services produced but also the distribution of their benefits and prospects for overall growth. The significance of technological choices made in the course of development extends beyond economics to social structure and political processes as well, and the growing interest in finding and implementing appropriate technologies reflects at least an implicit recognition of the essential role of technology in development policy (Eckaus, 1977:5).

Because the use of any particular technology is not an end in itself, the criterion of appropriateness for the choice of technology transferred must be found in the goals of the basic-needs approach to development. These goals are concerned not only with the volumes of output and income generated by an economy but also with the way such output and income are produced and distributed among the population. The basic-needs goals include, as well, particular patterns of national political change and independence.

Technology transfer is a powerful means of international policy. It serves as a means of projecting national influence and power onto the international arena. As a result, an increasing number of Third World countries have been advocating technology policies that promote development and greater national autonomy. But a careful formulation of technology policy is as important as development planning itself. Good plans can be ineffective if technology is insufficient in quantity, inappropriate in quality or undisciplined in its applications (Goulet, 1977b:167). As such, the acquisition and transfer of technology must be limited to appropriate technology. Significant efforts should be made by the developed countries to give access on improved terms to modern technology and the adaptation of that technology, as appropriate, to specific economic, social and ecological conditions and varying stages of development in less-developed countries.

The ability to make independent technological choices, to adapt and improve upon chosen techniques and products and eventually to generate new technology endogenously are essential aspects of the process of development. The process may be described as the accumulation of technological capacity; it is at least as important to economic development as the accumulation of capital.

The use of appropriate technology to satisfy basic needs is a national endeavour. Basic needs and the call for the transfer of appropriate technology are not just fads. They are no more, but also no less, than a stage in the thinking and responses to the challenges presented by development over the last twenty-five years (Streeten, 1979c:28).

To satisfy basic needs is an objective with high priority. As a development strategy, satisfying basic needs through the transfer of appropriate technology is even of higher priority. The accomplishment of this development framework places considerable emphasis on the concept of self-reliance that is collective in nature. The required global assistance must, however, be complementary to the policies being pursued in the developing nations. Technology and resource transfers, therefore, must not only be appropriate but mandatory. This means that within the context of basic-needs development, appropriate technology transfers from the rich nations to the poor nations must not depend on the uncertain generosity of the rich nations, but be based on some internationally accepted measure of the needs of the poor nations.

Some skeptics maintain that integration into any international economic order in which advanced capitalist economies dominate is inconsistent with technology transfer to meet basic needs of the poor in developing countries. They point to the People's Republic of China as a nation that, until recently, isolated itself from the evils of the international economic system and at the same time advocated that nations should shut themselves off from nefarious outside influences. But developing countries are not in a position to isolate themselves. Moreover, any such isolation would be counterproductive to the necessary technology transfers required to implement a successful basic-needs policy. Also, many developing countries are former colonies whose resources were raped and exploited both by the colonisers and by private transnational enterprises with little or no benefit to the said developing countries. Many Third World leaders, therefore, share the point of view that the transfer of resources and technology from developed nations for basic-needs development represents nothing more than repatriation.

This is an important issue because it is with some passion that Third World leaders share this view of repatriation. Further evidence of this feeling can be gleaned from the many recent nationalisations and increased tax levies that have been placed on multinational enterprises in the Third World. Increasingly, Third World leaders have been devoting more attention to changing the terms of foreign operations within their economies; nationalising ownership and top management; setting more precise conditions concerning participation, conservation, labour, investment and other aspects of foreign commercial activities to prevent further economic exploitation. But despite these attempts at direct intervention in the workings of their economies, numerous Third World leaders now believe that only if there is a basic change in the international economic order will the appropriate technology and sufficient resources flow to their countries to overcome some of the chronic disabilities of their economies (Wriggins and Adler-Karlsson, 1978:38).

So there is recognition of the need for interdependence, an interdependence that is in the form of a partnership based on interlocking economic systems and yet one in which the collective self-reliance of the developing countries is recognised and respected as a central emphasis in the transfer of appropriate technology to meet the basic needs of the majority of the population of the Third World. There is growing recognition that so long as the framework of a country's policy is appropriate—that is, the provision of basic needs is being pursued—the transfer of appropriate technology can improve resource allocation and efficiency without damage to balance of payments or national integrity. Countries that have effectively controlled technology transfers have done well. In contrast, autarkic policies have often led to slow growth and heavy dependence on aid with a concomitant impairment of independence (Hughes, 1980:20).

The provision of basic needs through the transfer of appropriate technology are two important objectives that would tend to make more resources available domestically and possibly internationally (Streeten, 1977:11). In the past, however, the transfer of technology to developing nations was facilitated primarily through transnational corporations and multilateral financial institutions. Yet, only a small proportion of projects showed any attempts to grapple with the technological problems involved (Dunkerley, 1977:36–39). Direct involvement, particularly that of the multilateral financial institutions such as the World Bank, in the formulation, implementation, supervision and assessment of a large number and variety of projects in developing nations provides these institutions with a unique opportunity to make major contributions to the transfer and promotion of more appropriate technologies, especially as it relates to basic needs (Dunkerley, 1977:36–39). This, therefore, should be advocated as a part of the policy of transnational corporations and multilateral financial institutions. A basic-needs strategy that is pursued through technology that is inappropriate is doomed to failure, irrespective of who finances it.

Bearing that in mind, the developing nations must develop criteria for the selection of technologies to be transferred to maximise the return from such technology. Within the framework of basic-needs satisfaction, the questions to be asked of any technology transferred are (1) does it directly or indirectly contribute to the satisfaction of such basic needs as food, clothes, shelter, health, education, transportation or communication and (2) does it produce goods or services accessible to those most in need? (Galtung, 1980:19–24; Helleiner, 1979:84–97).

Moreover, the purpose of laying down criteria for the selection and development of transferred technology is to broaden the base of decision making in this field. This is crucial for any progress in the field of development. The relative weight given to these criteria will, of course, vary from country to country and over time, but by making the criteria explicit it ensures that at least some consideration is given to each. Furthermore, the developed criteria will ensure the promotion of self-reliance. There is a very important qualitative difference between, say, ignoring completely the extent to which a technology builds self-reliance and considering the factor of self-reliance by giving it low or high weight but conceding that the technology chosen does not meet the criteria (Galtung, 1979:43–51).

Obviously, the development of such criteria would suggest a much more interventionist policy on the part of governments in the developing nations and in general a more selective policy toward technology transfer from abroad. The essential thrust is the ability to make technological choices that are in harmony with the development strategy being pursued and eventually to generate new technology endogenously. The process can be described as the accumulation of technological capacity. It is at least as important to economic development as the accumulation of capital. Reliance on technology developed in the advanced countries keeps the LDCs in a state of neocolonial technological dependency. As a result, many LDCs are now concerned with enhancing their internal technology capabilities by expending a much larger portion of their income for domestic research and development rather than paying for imported know-how. From the viewpoint of logic, this objective seems to reject the whole concept of technology transfer. This objective has been stated in LDCs' discussions concerning the inadequacies of the present system and, hence, gives further ammunition for arguments in favour of a New International Economic Order (NIEO) (Leff, 1979:94–95).

Undoubtedly, the best way to broaden the range of available technologies is, of course, to develop new technologies whenever the technology that is actually available is not appropriate. In principle, it is desirable that all technologies be conceived and developed in the countries in which they will be applied, which would diminish the perverse effects of inappropriate technology transfer (ILO, 1978:7–8). As such, the absolute level of research-and-development expenditures in LDCs should be increased in order that technological capacity may also increase. Increased technological capacity in turn increases productivity, which in turn has a positive impact on economic development. Developing local technology implies the need to internalize the technological dimension as part of an autonomous decision-making process by selective technological de-linking and by defining priorities for technological self-reliance (Ernst, 1981:467).

Technological self-reliance should cover the ability to generate, to adapt and to use technological systems to meet basic human needs and the ability to choose and control the areas of partial technological dependence, which will remain unavoidable in the LDCs for quite some time (Ernst, 1981:467). However, some degree of technological knowledge is required for this criterion of technological self-reliance to be satisfied (Little, 1982:237). Technological mastery is necessary for the efficient use of existing technology and for the development of further technological capacity. This is essentially the position of the "technologist school" with respect to technology policies for LDCs (Gillis et al., 1983:205). Original indigenous appropriate technology cannot be created if there is no technological mastery or technological capacity. Moreover, indigenous technology development is good business, at least in the long run, and the LDCs should attempt to capture the benefits deriving therefrom.

THE NEW INTERNATIONAL ECONOMIC ORDER

The concept of a NIEO is one embodying institutional arrangements that promote the economic and social progress of the developing countries in the context of an expanding world economy. It is a framework of rules and institutions regulating the relations among sovereign nations.

The fundamental elements of the approach toward an NIEO are threefold (Hope, 1979a:14). First, and most fundamental, measures are being sought to reduce and eventually eliminate, the economic dependence of developing countries on developed country enterprises in the production and trade of developing countries, thus allowing them to exercise full control over their natural resources. A second element is that of promoting the accelerated development of the economies of developing countries on the basis of self-reliance. Third, appropriate institutional changes are being sought to introduce some measure of global management of resources in the long-term interests of mankind.

The NIEO therefore stands for a new way of ordering the international economic system to bring about improved terms of trade between the present-day centre and periphery countries (in other words, the First World and the Third World countries); more control by the periphery over the world economic cycles that pass through them; and increased and improved trade among the periphery countries themselves (Galtung, 1980:29–30).

The NIEO concept has emerged primarily because of the defects of the existing international economy that perpetuates poverty and inequality, between countries and within countries (Abdel-Fadil et al., 1977:205). This economic crisis, which is centred in the major developed market economy countries, has adversely affected the economies of both developed and developing countries. Indeed, many of the poorer developing countries are facing a drastic deterioration in their economic positions. The economic crisis has therefore made even more urgent the implementation of effective international policies for development. At the same time, the concern of many of the developed countries for assured supplies of essential raw materials can be expected to make them more responsive than hitherto to the negotiation of new development policies.

The results of these concerns have been the wider recognition of the need for radical changes in the framework of international economic relations and, hence, have made changes in the framework more likely to be effectuated than heretofore.

The NIEO that the developing countries seek is intended to facilitate a direct attack on the central issue of widespread poverty. But it is generally felt that such an order could be without any impact at all on the majority of people in many developing countries unless those countries installed national arrangements to optimise their gains from an improved external regime and to bring about an equitable internal distribution of an increasing national product. However, it is recognised that many of the measures that are required to improve the internal economic order depend upon improved international arrangements in trade and finance (Ramphal, 1978:94).

Without improved internal arrangements and the required cooperation between developed and developing countries, then, there would be no complementarity with respect to meeting the objectives of the NIEO. As applied to the NIEO, the principle of complementarity means that something other than a mere redistribution of resources among nations is required. It means that all of the elements of the NIEO, internal and external must be achieved by close cooperation among the developed and developing countries with as much emphasis as possible on self-reliance.

Self-reliance must be the cornerstone of the NIEO. It means that the developing countries must do as much as possible for themselves on the basis of their own resources. Also, it must mean that collectively the developing countries must exploit every possible advantage for maximising the positive effects of the NIEO by cooperation among themselves. Self-reliance is taken here to mean autonomy of decision making and full mobilisation of a society's own resources under its own initiative and direction. It also means rejection of the principle of exploitative appropriation of others' resources.

Collective self-reliance is an extension of the concept of self-reliance so as to embrace truly cooperative relations among self-respecting mobilised societies. In other words, it is self-reliance reinforced by collective solidarity. Its concern is the enhancement of Third World productive forces, surplus generation and the power to carry forward development strategies in its own interest and for its own benefit. For this it is necessary to break with the components of the international system that generate or strengthen dependency and strengthen links with partners who share the principle of collective effort toward the attainment of the legitimate aspirations of each other and of mankind (Oteiza and Rahman, 1978:445–56).

This emphasis on self-reliance implies a striving to make relations between developed and less developed countries reflect genuine interdependence and international economic justice rather than continued dependence of the less-developed nations. To the extent that developed nations translate their affirmation of interdependence into more equitable international structures, there should be no fundamental conflict between self-reliant development and increased international economic cooperation through the NIEO.

The most important element of self-reliance in the developing nations (the South) is the formulation of concepts and policies of development based on their own socioeconomic realities rather than on ideas inherited from developed nations (the North). Developing nations have much to learn from the experience of developed nations. However, imitation will prove disastrous because the development strategy will reflect the policies of other nations. The relevance and importance of a self-reliant development policy are no longer questioned by policymakers in developing nations. A self-reliant development policy could give a great deal of impetus to the economies of the Third World countries and, in that sense, it could constitute the most dynamic element in the global strategy for development implied in the concept of an NIEO. The NIEO is intended to replace the current economic order. It is not a static concept but a dynamic and evolving process. Its defining characteristic is the attempt to eliminate economic injustice by equalising economic opportunity, conducive to unfolding productive capacities capable of responding to basic needs in all parts of the world (Hope, 1982b:163–76).

The concepts of beyond dependence and toward self-reliance define the striving toward the NIEO more than any specific international demand or resolution. But, though the formulation of NIEO objectives are subject to change and evolution, the NIEO itself will stay. A future without a NIEO is not conceivable (Laszlo et al., 1978:xxv). Moreover, an NIEO has become more urgent in view of the greater, deeper and more drastic deterioration that the world economic situation has undergone in the last few years (Castro, 1983:23).

EVOLUTIONARY NOTION OF DEVELOPMENT: TOWARD AN INTEGRATED STRATEGY

There can be little doubt that a thorough survey of opinion on the problem of development policy would show that at the end of the 1960s and at the beginning of the 1970s a new consensus began to emerge. Like most new approaches, it arose not in a vacuum but in response to the demonstrable failure of past beliefs and practices—beliefs and practices that were deemed necessary at the time for the continuation of the evolution into the realm of sustained economic growth and industrialisation (Healey, 1972:792).

Business cannot continue as usual in the process toward

development. Development policies that should have contributed to a more equitable distribution of income have served merely as additional instruments for increasing the wealth and power of developed nations. As such, the transfer of appropriate technology for the provision of basic needs becomes important and necessary. However, provision of basic needs and the transfer of appropriate technology still remain formidable tasks, though they are attainable within the context of the NIEO. The concept of basic needs brings to any development strategy a heightened concern with meeting the consumption needs of the Third World. But it is not a welfare concept nor is it a distinct development strategy in itself (Haq, 1980:11–14). It is a major objective of development that can be achieved only if the appropriate technology exists.

A strategy of integrated development embracing appropriate technology transfer, basic needs and the NIEO focuses on increasing cooperative relations among Third World nations and reducing their collective dependence on the developed nations. Its emphasis is on selective coordination of economic activities for maximising the provision of basic needs through the NIEO. Collective self-reliance, as stated before, is a necessary extension of national self-reliance for almost all Third World countries, both in terms of creating interdependent relationships with similar economies and of improving the economic exchange with the developed nations. However, as pointed out before, it cannot be a substitute for national strategies for self-reliance.

The kind of New Internal Economic Order needed to ensure that it is beneficial to the majority, rather than the elite, of Third World countries is one based on principles of self-reliant development. Bread and justice are most fully realised in societies committed to self-reliance (McGinnis, 1979:257). Thus, self-reliant development rejects concentrating national resources on the rich in the hope that something might trickle down. Instead, self-reliant development concentrates directly on those at the bottom and their basic needs. It is a model of development that emphasises meeting the basic human needs of the masses of people in a country through strategies geared to the particular human and natural re-

sources, values and traditions; and through strategies maximising the collective efforts of people within each country
and among Third World countries (McGinnis, 1979:261).
The conceptual framework of self-reliance focuses, therefore, on four elements. The first element pertains to basic human needs. This means attacking poverty directly and not
through the trickle-down process. In other words, it means
giving priority to the provision of food, shelter, housing, education, health care and jobs, at the least.

The second element relates to maximisation of the use of
local resources and values through the educational system as
appropriate to the needs, resources and values of the people.
It entails, therefore, the development of individuals as well
as nations. Education should be used to meet the basic needs
of individuals to receive a foundation of knowledge, attitudes, values and skills on which to build a later life for the
benefit of themselves and society. This element of self-reliance can be regarded as creative self-reliance. It is not self-
reliance in the sense of cutting off links completely from the
world but self-reliance in the sense of being self-confident as
nations to base development on their own cultural values. It
implies reliance by a nation on its own thinking and on its
own value system without being defensive or apologetic (Haq,
1976:71–75).

The third element in the framework deals with participation of the masses in the development thrust—the willing and
active participation of the masses in the development of the
nation-state in which they reside. Such participation requires
that the masses not only share in the distribution of the benefits of development, be they the material benefits of increased output or other benefits considered to enhance the
quality of life, but that they share also in the task of creating
those benefits.

The fourth and final element in the conceptual framework
pertains to the issue of interdependence or collective self-
reliance. That is, technical cooperation among Third World
countries for their individual as well as collective development. Undoubtedly, collective self-reliance and growing cooperation among developing countries will further strengthen

their role in the New International Economic Order. Cooperation among these countries is aimed at generating or adapting knowledge needed for a socially relevant endogenous self-sustained development process to avoid the blind or forced transfer of inadequate technology. Moreover, the expansion of the capacity of Third World countries to generate and adapt knowledge through a cooperative effort can contribute toward a more equitable world order in which choices are greater, solutions are better adapted to the specific historical circumstances of different countries, and dependence is decreased. Furthermore, cooperation among developing countries can also contribute to fill the vacuum of regional and interregional links among Third World countries. This vacuum is the result of the historical colonial heritage of exclusive links later on maintained through a world order that has not allowed the emergence of alternative patterns more suitable than traditional centre-periphery ones for Third World countries. The collective self-reliance approach to development, therefore, implies a de-linking from those components of the international system in which a balanced relationship cannot be established and a re-linking among Third World countries with whom a balanced relationship may be attained.

The foregoing puts the issue of self-reliance in conceptual perspective. Primary emphasis is placed by the Third World countries on genuine cooperation, which is regarded as an egalitarian form of partnership in which nationally based effort and the benefits of a joint undertaking in the short and long term are shared evenly among participating countries. Cooperation is seen as a partnership in which parties have equal status irrespective of their relative economic, political or military strengths, where efforts and benefits are shared in accordance with their abilities and needs. It is, above all, a "solidarity contract" to contribute to the fulfillment of each party's legitimate aspirations, and to unite against forces opposing these aspirations and seeking to increase dependency (Oteiza and Rahman, 1978:450; Murphy, 1983:72).

In effect, the goal is to increase the level of interdependence within the Third World, not only to achieve immediate welfare gains from increased trade and specialisation, but also to improve the quality and credibility of common bargaining positions against the industrial countries. An improved bargaining position would presumably emerge from the fact that more collective self-reliance would gradually provide the Third World with a feasible alternative in any confrontation with the rich countries. But even apart from this, there is no doubt that efforts to increase cooperation make a great deal of sense. The immediate gains may not be huge and the gains might not be equitably distributed but over the long term the importance of such actions could surely be important. This is particularly true if the industrial nations remain in recession or if they turn inward or if they begin actively to seek substitutes for many of the Third World's exports (Rothstein, 1977:261–62).

As such, the self-reliance model has clear and important functions. It remains an alternative development strategy that— even if it is very difficult to implement in its extreme form of de-linking the South from the North—can at least provide guidance for the kinds of changes that are required to eliminate underdevelopment. As an ideal type, it can provide direction for partial strategies. Naturally, the attractiveness of this alternative increases as the limitations of the export-led approach become more evident or the negotiations about the implementation of the NIEO program remain deadlocked (Sauvant, 1981:19).

The whole theory of self-reliance hinges on one fundamental hypothesis: that together resources constitute a reservoir, now partly drained away, partly misdirected and largely underutilised, that is sufficient for the satisfaction of basic human material needs all over the world. It is a complex strategy—needing both built-in dynamism and firm institutional foundations—calculated to generate and implement clusters of collective schemes and a pattern of regeneration through one's own efforts.

The recognition of a strategy of integrated development is very important at both the macro and micro levels. At the macro level the strategy must be so designed to ensure consistency between the basic-needs indicators and transfers derived from the NIEO. At the micro level, there must be analysis to identify potential alternative policies and to choose those contributing most to the unity and efficiency of providing basic needs and transferring appropriate technology in the context of the NIEO. The NIEO deals essentially with the relations between industrialised and developing countries at the global level. It is thus a macro approach to the problem of development. The basic-needs approach, on the other hand, is a micro approach. It goes down to the level of the individual human being and, therefore, sees development in terms of fulfillment of basic needs at the individual level.

The provision of basic needs and the transfer of appropriate technology are now recognised as fundamental to the development process. There is further recognition that this should be attempted in concert with the NIEO. There now seems to be general agreement that the meeting of basic needs of the poor should become the core of development planning and policy (Ghai et al., 1977:14). Furthermore, discussions on basic needs emphasise its dynamic nature. Basic-needs development is seen as evolving over time, within the NIEO, in line with the growth of the economy and the aspirations of the people. It is regarded as the primary output of any integrated development strategy where horizontal rather than vertical interdependence is expected to be achieved, as indicated in the chart.

Vertical interdependence is a relationship of inequality with the controlling element at the top and others on the bottom as seen in the present international economic order. On the other hand, horizontal interdependence, as would be brought about in the NIEO, is based on equality and is concerned with both present and future generations. Numerous Third World leaders, therefore, now recognise the necessity for a change in the present international economic order. They are seeking a larger share of the final consumer price of products made from their raw materials and increased influence on how the world economy is shaped and managed. Whereas the earlier efforts to obtain additional economic resources from First World countries involved bilateral negotiations by individual Third World states with sources of funds or with specific companies in the First World, the new activism on behalf of

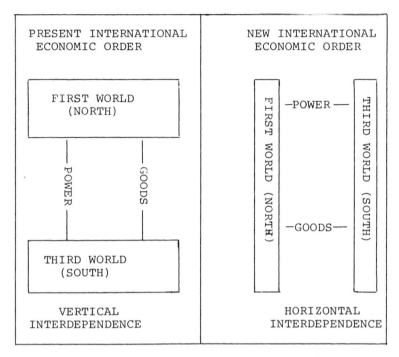

Source: Adapted from McGinnis, 1979:51.   Copyright 1979 by
    James B. McGinnis.   Used by permission from Paulist Press,
    Ramsey, N. J.

a changed economic order calls for joint efforts by members
of Third World states (Wriggins and Adler-Karlsson, 1978:38).

The future of Third World unity and the success of Third
World leaders in effecting structural changes in the international economic system also depends upon the extent to which
divisive forces in the Third World can be contained. There is
a widening of the economic gap among the developing nations; in addition, there is an increasing differentiation in terms
of political ideologies and military strength. On the one hand,
there has been an increase in the number of Third World
governments that have a pronounced radical-leftist political
philosophy while, on the other hand, in a large number of
Third World countries liberal-democratic governments have
been replaced by authoritarian regimes run by an alliance

between the militiary and the bureaucracy (Islam, 1979:193). Apparently, though, the most important differentiation existing in the Third World is in the economic area and this is due to the increasing disparity in the income levels between the middle-income and poorer countries (Islam, 1979:194).

Dependency theory, though, tends to overstate the role of external influences and consequently minimises the internal factors affecting the development of more equitable domestic economic, social and political systems. But a reduction of dependence on the North requires not only the achievement of better international bargains but also better management of local resources and significant social and economic changes within the Third World. These changes are essential for the political viability of those Third World regimes that do not depend on force to stay in power. However, dependency theory clearly has contributed to the increased awareness of Third World leaders of the relative strengths and weaknesses of their positions and has certainly heightened their desires for greater autonomy in international economic affairs. Dependency theory is one of the most important factors contributing to the growing sense of self-reliance that is prompting Third World nations to seek more influence over their political and economic destinies (Erb, 1975:140).

The dependency perspective assumes that the development of a national or regional unit can only be understood in connection with its historical insertion into the worldwide political-economic system which emerged with the wave of European colonisations of the world. The global system is thought to be characterised by the unequal but the combined development of its various components. Both development and underdevelopment are seen as aspects of the same phenomenon. Both are linked functionally and, therefore, interact and condition each other mutually. This results in the division of the world between industrial or "centre" countries and developing or "periphery" countries. The centre is viewed as capable of dynamic development responsive to internal needs, and as the main beneficiary of the global links. On the other hand, the periphery is seen as having a reflex type of development that is constrained by its incorporation into the global system and that results from its adaptation to the requirements of the expansion of the centre (Valenzuela and Valenzuela, 1981:25).

Dependency theory stresses the significance of the manner in which the internal and external structural components are connected. External variables are reinforced by internal factors and it is through this interplay that the Third World would like to continue to develop as long as they are equal partners in that process and exploitation ceases. It means then that the Third World nations are seeking greater equity in international economic relations and, particularly, in the decision-making process affecting their development. They would like to see the creation of a new world order with a NIEO as the *sine qua non* in that structure for their progress.

The call for a NIEO expresses both a criticism of the existing order and a crusade for justice and welfare. It is put forward collectively by countries that constitute a large majority of the United Nations membership and it goes beyond mere complaints and claims based on a certain rationale of a concept and interpretation of the world economy and an emerging vision of a more desirable world order. In effect, a call for a NIEO implies a model of a structured world economy that performs in a particular way and can be restructured to perform in a different way, with a different pattern of benefits and costs to the various groups involved. Thus the NIEO concept denounces the existing order on the private and the public side (Reubens, 1981:6–7). It suggests, rather, conscious and collaborative efforts to shape certain aspects of international relationships by employing new institutions and new thinking.

From the foregoing analysis, it seems that the Third World nations have some valid arguments about the present world economic system. However, it is also quite obvious that there are limits to equality and to the extent to which the countries of the North are willing to accommodate such Third World initiatives. But the dialogue must continue. A compromise must be reached. The countries of the North must make concessions to the countries of the South. The countries of the South currently have a greater capacity to disrupt the present international order in ways that harm both the North and the South, but harm the North more because they have more to lose. There is a probability that desperation arising out of poverty could lead to instability within the individual countries of the South; regional conflicts in the developing world; and a general sense of insecurity and tension in the world at large. Therefore, it would seem to be in the wider interest of the Northern nations to mitigate this. However, it needs to be acknowledged also that an inequitable internal regime is a poor basis on which to seek international equity and the developing nations must accept this fact (Islam, 1981:248–49).

International development policy has thus reached a crossroads where an entirely new strategy orientation is required. One that would provide adequate protection for developing countries against the adverse short-term consequences of economic instability in developed nations, one that also would promote the longer-term structural changes necessary for accelerating the economic and social progress of the Third World (Corea, 1981:48–55).

New development strategies, based on a fuller mobilisation of domestic resources, are required. A more self-reliant industrialisation policy and an increased emphasis on meeting basic human needs will result in significant shifts in the pattern of industrial production and in an increased use of indigenous technologies.

What makes the basic-human-needs approach of considerable current importance is that it has moved from an abstract concept to an explicit policy objective endorsed by major donor countries such as the United States and by multilateral institutions such as the World Bank. Former Secretary of State Cyrus Vance gave the United States endorsement at the Organisation for Economic Cooperation and Development in June 1977 and since then, basic needs has been an accepted policy of the United States government as reflected in the Foreign Assistance Act of 1978. However, the countries of the North see the basic-needs objectives as a counterpolicy to the demands by the developing nations for a NIEO. But the objectives of a basic-needs policy should not be presented as demands for internal policy changes in the developing nations to substitute for changes in the international economic structure. Rather, reforms in the international economy that enable a larger number of developing countries to participate effectively in the world's trade and investment flows can be complementary to domestic and donor efforts to foster more equitable growth in developing nations (Leipziger, 1981:263–64).

The central message being conveyed here is that basic needs and the New International Economic Order represent potentially complementary strategies for dealing positively with the global problems of poverty and inequality. A basic-needs policy focuses on the domestic dimension of these problems and its counterpart, NIEO, concentrates on the international aspects. The two strategies are interrelated to the extent that domestic and international conditions interact. The NIEO is a call for a revision of the rules and institutions regulating the relations between sovereign nations, and meeting basic needs is one important objective that this framework should serve.

This then is the essence of another development—an integrated strategy that is geared to the satisfaction of basic needs through the transfer and use of technology that is appropriate and one where collective self-reliance is emphasised within an international economy that stresses global equity rather than dependence.

FINANCING DEVELOPMENT IN DEVELOPING NATIONS

Despite the shifting emphasis, contrasting perceptions and the many development fashions over the years, the financing of development in the developing nations has always posed a problem. The peculiar problem of finance is fundamentally one of using the fiscal system to capture resources for the purposes of the development programme.

Regardless of the development philosophy being pursued, any government development programme costs money and requires the raising of revenue. Indeed, short of war, it can be one of the most expensive activities in which governments today engage. Hence, the primary issue is that of the mobilisation of resources to an optimal point for the achievement of socioeconomic development. Financing ultimately determines whether the adjustment process taking place in the LDCs will be successful. But the actual method of financing depends on both the needs of countries and on the likely availability and cost of financing from all sources given the widely differing needs of the developing countries for finance. The subject of development finance relates to the provision of real resources to raise the level of real output and living standards in developing nations. The growth of output, as discussed before, is not the only goal of economic policy in developing nations. Rather, it is complementary to the other socioeconomic goals and must be considered in the planning process for the acquisition of resources for financing development.

Tax Policy

The most salient characteristic of taxation is its compulsory nature. There is no *quid pro quo* relationship of taxes paid and benefits received by the citizenry. So far, all attempts to establish a relationship between taxes paid and benefits received by the citizenry have failed. There is no way of ascertaining the true benefits. If public goods are relatively "pure" and the exclusion principle does not apply, there are no discrete outputs that are appropriable by individuals. However, the generally accepted goals of taxation are (1) efficient resource allocation, (2) full employment with price stability, (3) a satisfactory distribution of income, and (4) a high stable rate of economic growth. These goals have to be judged by certain criteria as to how they are fulfilled.

Four general criteria can be developed to evaluate taxes. These are allocational efficiency, equity, administrative feasibility and revenue productivity. The first is concerned with the economic effects of taxation on the pattern of resource allocation. Equity refers to different taxes and how each tax redistributes income and wealth among the citizens in such a way as to narrow the gap between the poor and rich. Administrative feasibility encompasses the problems dealing with how efficiently a particular tax can be administered. And finally, revenue productivity deals with the ability of a tax to maximise government revenues. These are standard criteria used in taxation theory for the purpose of evaluating various taxes. However, while the criteria for evaluating various taxes are generally agreed upon, there is no agreement on an ideal tax system for all countries. A country's tax system must be reviewed periodically as development proceeds. Dependence on various taxes for revenues must be modified as the economy of a country changes. The aim should always be a tax system that will be adequate, flexible and in harmony with the emerging pattern of economic activity. Furthermore, these general criteria for appraising a tax system may be in conflict with each other. Neutrality may be in conflict with revenue productivity criteria, and revenue productivity may be in conflict with equity criteria.

In examining the literature on tax policy in LDCs it is found that almost all of the studies seem to agree that the tax system must transfer resources from the private to the public sector so that the public sector will have the ability to carry out those functions that are basic to the role of government as well as those functions that are related to the development of the countries. The tax system must also induce a transfer of resources within the private sector from low-priority uses toward high-priority uses. Taxes put resources in the hands of governments, and these resources can be used for carrying out certain investment programs that are supposed to be productive to the economy, especially in the long run.

In the early stages of the economic development of the United Kingdom and the United States, their fiscal structure as a whole favoured the act of accumulation and capital formation and discriminated against the act of consumption. The economic development of these countries has been brought about largely by the efforts of a dynamic private enterprise; and to enable it to plough back its increasing incomes into investment, the structure of taxation was made highly regressive and the fiscal structure tended to redistribute the national income in favour of the investors and savers.

In the LDCs, the public sector is obliged to play an increasingly important role in accelerating development and it may not be reasonable to finance the development outlay of the public sector by depending entirely on regressive taxes. In a democratic type of country, such a distribution of tax burden, apart from being contrary to the sense of justice and equity of a democratic society, may also create social discontent that may hinder the process of economic development. Besides, there exists a much greater concentration of income and wealth in the hands of a very small proportion of the population in a developing country, and the process of economic development will tend to magnify these concentrations. Some of these concentrations of income and wealth emanate from nonentrepreneurial sources such as rent and interest, and the persons in possession of such wealth and income have no tradition of saving and productive investment but they are inclined to dissipate their incomes into nonfunctional consumption and unproductive investment. Therefore, tax policy in the developing country as an instrument of development finance for the public sector has to be geared effectively to the taxation of nonentrepreneurial incomes, providing at the same time adequate incentive to the private sector undertaking useful production and essential investment (Tripathy, 1964:96).

Though in the early stages of the economic development of the United Kingdom and the United States the tax structure was predominantly regressive with the tax system completely dependent on outlay taxes, the position has been fundamentally reversed in modern times, and the taxes on income and wealth are more important in their tax structure than the taxes on outlay.

Public savings in the developing countries are bound to remain small if their tax-income ratios are not substantially raised. The existing tax structure in many developing countries results in a rapid growth of tax revenues unless there are frequent changes in coverage and rates of taxation. During the period 1972–1976 it was found that the average tax ratio in developing countries was 16.1 percent compared to 15.1 percent in 1969–1971 and 13.6 percent in 1966–1968 (Tait et al., 1979; Chelliah et al., 1975; Chelliah, 1971). But in spite of this general increase in tax ratios, the average level of taxation in these countries is still considerably less than in developed countries. The primary reason for this difference is, of course, the wide difference in per capita income levels. When a comparison is made between the two groups of countries, per capita income differences are clearly seen to be associated with tax level differences (Chelliah, 1971:280–82). Tax ratios measure the level of taxation in a country. This is usually judged in terms of the ratio of taxes to some measure of national product. What elements should be included in the numerator and the denominator of the ratio depend on what aspect of the governmental role one wishes this ratio to reflect or signify and what one intends to show by international comparisons of tax levels. The standard approach has been to use the ratio of all taxes and taxlike charges to gross national product at market prices. Hence, the overall tax ratio shows the proportion of national income that is "compulsorily" transferred from private hands to the government sector for public purposes. As such, the ratio gives an idea of the division of responsibilities between the public and the private sectors and the degree of control that the government can potentially exercise over the disposition of purchasing power in the economy (Chelliah, 1971:258).

Tax ratios and changes in them over time are matters that are subject to control by governments. Nevertheless, the changes in tax ratios brought about in different developing countries are partly dependent on major characteristics of the economy that have a bearing on taxable capacity. Tax ratios have been widely regarded as an index of the size of the public sector, and many studies have attempted to explain the variations in the size of the public sector as reflected in tax ratio differences between different countries as well as over time. These studies have tried to discover whether there is any measurable relationship between economic characteristics including the existing level of development and tax ratios. The majority of the studies have been in the nature of cross-section analysis.

The pioneering study of tax ratio variations, explained by different economic and sociopolitical factors, was done by Martin and Lewis (1956). They concluded that the proportion of national income spent on basic public services varies not so much with income as with the "progressiveness" of the rulers or electorate of the state. Several other works duplicated these results and added new variables.

It can be concluded that, "conceptually, the tax ratio or share of national income appropriated by the government can be determined by four broad groups of factors" (Chelliah, 1971:292). On the demand for government services side, there may be two groups of factors: the need for services arising out of "objective" conditions and the preferences of the people and the leaders as between public and private services, including the institutional arrangements arising from them. On the side of raising resources or supply of funds, two operative factors may be suggested. The first one being the ability of the people to pay taxes and the second factor being the ability of the government to collect taxes.

However, while a simple comparison of tax ratios gives some indication of the relative levels of taxation in various areas, any inference on tax performance or effort based merely on such a comparison fails to take into account the fact that some countries are more favourably placed to levy taxes. That is, they can be said to have greater taxable capacity than others. It has been pointed out that the successful measurement of taxable capacity used in many studies depends critically on the *a priori* justification of the explanatory variables as affecting only taxable capacity and not at all affecting either demands for higher public expenditures or willingness to tax. It is not surprising, therefore, that Richard Bird has argued quite convincingly that the distinction between "capacity" and "willingness" is a very fuzzy one and indeed "it is inherently extremely difficult to specify correctly any model of (usable) taxable capacity to quantify what Musgrave has called the 'tax handles' available to a country" (Bird, 1976:253).

Accepting, however, that something called "taxable capacity" exists, the next step is that of calculation of tax effort. Tax effort is defined as the ratio of the actual tax ratio in a particular country to the ratio that would be predicted on the basis of the taxable capacity concept. A tax effort ratio of less than one is usually taken to mean that the country exploits its estimated tax potential less than the average; in other words, that it has a preference for a level of taxation below the average or a low tax effort. Tax effort is a process that may take several forms, including reform of existing taxes, improvement in administration and introduction of new taxes. The indices of tax effort should not be used in a mechanistic way but should be considered useful additional information in judging the scope for more taxes.

The tax ratio and tax effort concepts discussed above are based on two sets of techniques for comparative analysis. One technique equates tax effort to the ratio of taxes (or revenues) to income. Such a straightforward comparison implicitly assumes total income to be the only relevant indicator of intercountry differences in taxable capacity. The second technique, a stochastic approach, gives markedly different results. It involves the assumption that the tax ratio (T/Y) is an appropriate reflection of taxable capacity if it is adjusted for intercountry variations in factors that are assumed to reflect intercountry differences in the size of the tax base and the ability to collect taxes. While clearly preferable to a straight tax ratio for comparative purposes, the stochastic approach has a number of methodological problems. In general, the aggregative regression approach does not allow a desirable examination of the kinds of explicit relationships between particular taxes and particular economic structure variables that would seem useful for purposes of making intercountry comparisons of taxable capacity and tax effort.

Bearing these facts in mind, Roy Bahl (1972) proceeded to develop an alternative method for making intercountry tax effort comparisons in which the tax effort index derived may be related to the intensity of use of specific taxes. He designated his methodology as the "representative tax system approach," and it involves application of average effective rates to a standard set of tax bases. This approach does allow an examination of marginal effects. Taxable capacity is defined in this approach as the total tax amount that would be collected if each country applied an identical set of effective rates to the selected tax bases, that is, as the yield of a representative tax system.

The application of the representative tax system approach gave a distribution that did not differ significantly from that obtained in the analyses employing the aggregate regression approach. However, three general observations can be pointed out. First, the level of taxable capacity responds most to changes originating in basic sector income. Second, the yield of a representative system is more responsive to a change in income generated in a particular sector if it is accompanied by a change in total income than if it reflects only a sectoral redistribution of some constant amount of income. Third, the criticism that tax effort indices and rankings vary erratically with changes in the estimating procedure used was not strengthened by the representative approach.

Other studies in recent years have attempted other approaches to measure what essentially seems to be tax ratios and tax efforts. However, tax effort studies and methodologies have not been immune from criticism. The International Monetary Fund (IMF) where most of these studies were conducted, pointed out that "due caution must be exercised in interpreting the tax effort indices" (IMF, 1974:164). Vito Tanzi noted with regard to tax structure development that clearly up to now the marriage between general theories and the statistical analysis carried on thus far to verify those theories has not taken place yet. He further stated that "the truth of the matter is that we still do not have an answer to the question of what kind of tax structure a country should have at a given stage of economic development" (Tanzi, 1974:62–63).

Richard Bird (1976) made five points that he considered to be his basic criticisms of the tax effort studies: (1) There is inadequate *a priori* justification for the use of the selected variables as measures of taxable capacity. (2) The data is very bad. These data problems are very serious, and no one can truthfully claim to be aware of all the biases they impart to the result. (3) Virtually all of the work that has been done on quantitative international comparisons is cross-sectional in nature; yet the policy inferences that are drawn from these works are invariably concerned with changes in particular areas. (4) The nature of the norms applied in tax effort analysis lend themselves to distortions. Further, the implicit norm in the usual use of the tax effort index may also be criticised as being proportional. (5) The conventional tax effort exercise lends itself too readily to misuse to be worth further attention at this stage of our knowledge. Despite these worthy criticisms, the general tendency has been to use these studies, particularly in the international lending agencies, as the background for policy decisions.

Apart from tax structure, tax effort and tax ratio studies, a significant amount of work has been done on tax incidence in developing countries. It seems that the major reason for this has been the desire to provide quantitative, and therefore supposedly definitive, support for particular policy positions—which usually means to demonstrate the case for a more progressive tax system.

The shifting assumptions used in those studies are the traditional ones. Indirect taxes were generally assumed to be shifted forward, and direct taxes unshifted. Corporate profits taxes were assumed to be shifted forward in various proportions, but no backward shifting was considered. The shifting assumptions adopted on property and wealth taxes varied. Some studies assumed no shifting while others allowed for some forward shifting of the property tax on rental property. The proportion of this tax that is assumed to be shifted forward varied greatly from study to study.

Three major reasons for making tax incidence studies can probably be distinguished. First, most studies wanted to analyse the redistribution of income through the fiscal system and concentrated on the effects of taxes on different income size classes of the population. They were concerned with vertical equity. A second group of incidence studies concentrated on the differential tax burden between the rural and the urban sectors and on the transfer of resources between these two sectors. This emphasis stems from concern with both horizontal equity and policy for development. The third category of studies was concerned with the horizontal equity between various geographical areas or between various ethnic components of a country. All of the studies favoured redistribution of income from the rich to the poor. A progressive tax system was also deemed a desirable feature of fiscal policy and, as such, results showing the redistribution effects of fiscal policy were welcomed even though the lowest income classes were often found to contribute a considerable fraction of their incomes in taxes, and those showing regressive taxes led to recommendations for the elimination of the regressivity.

Basically, both from a conceptual and statistical point of view, tax incidence studies are too questionable to bear the weight of interpretation that is sometimes put upon them. At most, properly constructed and heavily qualified incidence estimates can be a useful supplement to efforts to appraise and improve tax systems in developing countries: they cannot, however, provide a road map to the better world (Bird and De Wulf, 1973:677).

From the foregoing it is quite obvious that there are many problems associated with tax policy in developing countries. As such, interest in the study of tax policy in developing nations seems to have waned in recent years. There is now a greater concern with income distribution and attention has shifted from taxation to public expenditures. Moreover, the transience of many conclusions of tax theory and the pessimism about prospects for tax reform have also discouraged research on tax policy in developing nations (Jetha, 1981:448). As such, there is currently a great deal of misunderstanding and uncertainty about the usefulness of tax policies in developing nations.

What seems certain, however, is the fact that many developing nations have already made impressive progress in improving their tax gathering. Since 1976, though, tax ratios in developing nations have not increased and, although some obvious steps can be taken (making taxes more progressive and reducing evasion and arrears), the scope for raising taxation is less now than it was twenty years ago (World Bank, 1980:73). This is particularly true of the poorer nations even where foreign trade is a major share of output. Their tax administration is usually weaker, there is generally substantial unmarketed output and their taxable surplus accounts for a

smaller share of their gross national product (Bird, 1983:3–
14). This ultimately leads to attempts to mobilise other sources
of development finance.

The Role of Domestic Savings

Savings, or the formation of capital, is one of the important
prerequisites to economic development. The mobilisation of
savings has in recent years become a frequent recommenda-
tion for development policies. A macroeconomic approach is
often used indicating the amount of investment needed to increase the national output annually at a certain rate. If the
proposed amount needed for investment is based on a calculated rate of gross domestic savings, this will not be enough
to determine the amount of funds necessary for public and
private investments unless the sources of these funds are
identified. An overall estimate of resources expected to be
available for investment must be supplemented by an indication of the sources of saving. Only then can one project the
use of gross capital formation for investment in various areas.

Domestic savings can be divided into public sector savings
(government saving plus retained profits of public enterprises) and private sector savings. Public sector savings have
assumed growing importance as a source of development finance in the developing countries. During the past decade
public investment has been stepped up nearly everywhere and
the expectation that public sector savings will help in financing public investment is evidenced in most of the development plans. In these plans, estimates of financial requirements are divided into domestic sources and inflow of foreign
funds. In a number of countries, public sector savings have
been assigned a sizeable proportion of domestic resources.
Thus, the problem of public sector savings is closely related
not only to taxable capacity of the country but also to the trend
of current public sector expenditure.

The importance of a continuous and expanding flow of private savings for financing both private and public investments is recognised throughout the less-developed countries,
and the need to take measures aimed at increasing the rate of
private savings is stressed. Thus, the importance of raising the

rate of private savings for financing development is obvious, but the question is through what policies and mechanisms can this be achieved. This situation will vary from country to country and the financial organisation will have to be adapted to local conditions (Hope, 1980:260).

In essence, there is little meaning in discussing "mobilisation of savings" without specifying not only all the policy targets to be fulfilled but also the policy means to be used. Equalisation of income and equity considerations may be just as important in practical development policy as investments. We can only say, in general, that depending on the policy programme and the means to be used, it may be necessary to influence savings with respect to size as well as composition. With respect to development programmes, the task will invariably be to increase the size of domestic savings and accordingly to stimulate the propensity to save but nothing can be said in general concerning the composition of savings. In any case, we are interested in the possibilities of affecting both the size and the composition of savings.

Increases in gross domestic savings, or, more so, public sector savings, given the deteriorating private sector in LDCs, necessarily imply increases in revenues or decreases in public expenditures. In light of the current development thrust of the LDCs which is concomitant with increased public expenditure, the feasible and only alternative is that of increased revenues. Bearing in mind the structure of total revenue in LDCs, the conclusion emerges that increases in the savings of the public sector would have to be brought about through increased tax revenues. With respect to the private sector, there should be further encouragement of savings from households. This can be done through two mechanisms.

First, assurance should be given by governments against loss of savings from inflation. Or better still, a significant effort should be made by governments to curb inflation. A most important deterrent to household savings is inflation. Most households, particularly savers of small amounts, have no satisfactory means of protecting their savings from depreciation due to inflation. When prices have risen steadily the will to accumulate savings in the form of deposits, government bonds or life insurance is undermined or eventually destroyed. In Israel, for example, the introduction of special schemes linking the value of savings to the cost of living or the dollar exchange rate attracted a large amount of savings funds, much of it new.

The second mechanism relates to use of the interest rate. The savings rates of interest should be raised. A higher rate of interest will induce the public to further increase its savings and to hold more of its savings in the form of deposits and bonds, rather than in hoards of foreign exchange which is already very scarce in LDCs. Furthermore, higher rates of interest will tend to encourage much more economical use of capital and thus diminish the deficiency of resources for development. Households clearly prefer to hold their savings in the form of claims on financial institutions rather than in the form of direct claims on the government and corporate sectors. Hence, any further incentives provided by these financial institutions, in the form of higher interest rates, will tend to increase the volume of household savings (Hope, 1982c:386).

It must be pointed out again that in any increase in gross domestic savings, the majority of that increase would have to come from the public sector for reasons already stated, but the savings of central governments (excess of revenue over current expenditure) in LDCs have been extremely volatile.

The savings of central governments have an important role to play in the accumulation of both total public sector savings and gross domestic savings. This is so because of the increasing scarcity of funds from the international financial institutions. This increased savings performance will require careful budgetary management by central governments as well as a reduction in the dependence of public corporations on central governments for both current and capital transfers. The reduction of public corporations' dependence on the central governments would require that measures be taken to improve the net earnings of public enterprises. This would, among other things, require that these enterprises be managed efficiently and be allowed to charge prices that would enable them to earn profits that could then be invested in accordance with government policies as stipulated in the development plans.

Although data on savings is among the least reliable data around, it is possible to gauge the growth of savings in the LDCs as shown in table 2.1. As exhibited, for both the low-income and middle-income countries the savings rate has been increasing. By 1990, it is expected that the rate of savings for low-income countries would exceed 20 percent while for the middle-income countries the savings rate is expected to continue its marginal rate of increase.

However, given the general consensus that central government current revenue may decrease due to the decline in export earnings in LDCs coupled with the expanding role of state activity, it can be expected that in the next few years government savings will fall unless greater use is made of budgetary management and the tax structure or, better still, effective fiscal policy.

Fiscal policy is now widely recognised to be a potent instrument for achieving important economic and social objectives in developing countries. One of the primary objectives of fiscal policy in those countries is to raise the ratio of savings to national income so that the rate of net investment could be stepped up without the danger of inflation.

As the rate of private savings continues to decline and the role of the public sector expands, public savings undoubtedly assumes further importance and it becomes necessary to reorient fiscal policy to generate sizeable surpluses in the public sector.

In as much as the main sources of public sector savings are taxes and surpluses of public enterprises, it may be taken to

Table 2.1
Savings Rates of Developing Countries, 1961–1990
(Percentage of GDP, Current Prices)

Country Group	1961–1970	1976	1980	1985	1990
Low-Income Countries	14.7	15.7	18.7	19.8	21.2
Middle-Income Countries	18.8	23.1	23.2	23.8	24.5
All Developing Countries	17.0	21.9	22.4	23.1	24.0

Source: World Bank, World Development Reports (Washington, D.C.: World Bank, several years).

represent collective compulsory savings by the community, as distinguished from voluntary savings by households and private corporations. Public savings have a dual role to play. On the one hand, it constitutes a convenient source of finance for public investment and, on the other, it may serve to raise the rate of savings in the economy.

In the LDCs it appears that though domestic savings has been increasing it has borne no close determinable relationship to government revenue in the past. Saving has occurred, whenever it has occurred, more as a residue than as a result of conscious development planning to achieve a given rate of savings. For many of the developing nations, sudden and unforeseen increases in current expenditure results in negative savings in some years, while buoyancy in revenues or increases in tax collections, unaccompanied by an immediate rise in expenditure, produced a high rate of saving in other years. Fluctuations in revenues, brought about primarily through changes in export earnings, have also been responsible for wide variations in the rate of savings.

Since government revenues are subject to many complex factors and the level of government expenditure has to be determined on the basis of a multitude of considerations, it is perhaps inevitable that the rate of savings should fluctuate from year to year. However, what is really important is that governments must be able to save a fairly substantial proportion of their revenue over a period of years and they should consciously seek to raise this proportion in the succeeding periods so that the savings-investment gap can be reduced.

Foreign Aid

Foreign aid refers to flows of resources made on concessional terms to foreign governments either directly on a bilateral basis or indirectly through multilateral organisations. Foreign aid originated for three reasons. The first reason was that of a general concern for the well-being of the world's poor and the promotion of growth and development in the poor nations. The second reason was the United States' fear of communist expansionism, and the final reason was European imperial politics. In the last two cases, the ultimate intent was that of promoting a particular ideological and political framework in the sense that the granting of aid might tend to encourage the recipients to become friendly with and accept the ideological and political stance of the donors who hoped, in turn, to maintain a position of influence and control over the recipient countries.

Developing countries supplement savings by obtaining foreign aid. These resource inflows permit a less-developed country to undertake more investment than would be possible by relying on domestic savings alone. It has generally been advocated that the effectiveness of aid is usually measured in terms of its effect on growth, which could be expected subsequently to become self-sustaining. Chenery and Strout (1966) have argued that their examples support the theoretical conclusion that the achievement of a high rate of growth, even though it has to be initially supported by large amounts of external capital, is likely to be the most important element in the long-term effectiveness of assistance. The substantial increases in internal savings ratios that have been achieved in periods of strong growth demonstrate the rapidity with which aid-sustained growth can be transformed into self-sustained growth once rapid development has taken hold.

Griffin and Enos (1970a), on the other hand, have suggested that if anything, aid may have retarded development by leading to lower domestic savings, by distorting the composition of investment and thereby raising the capital/output ratio, by frustrating the emergence of an indigenous entrepreneurial class and by inhibiting institutional reforms. Instead of obtaining evidence for growth induced by aid, they have observed that the opposite hypothesis is closer to the truth and that, in general, foreign assistance is not associated with progress and, indeed, may deter it. If the growth that a nation achieves or fails to achieve is related to the assistance it receives, one finds that there is no support for the view that aid encourages growth.

Public opinion about foreign aid has fluctuated considerably during the past two decades. Hopes were at first high that financial aid would provide the necessary infrastructure of transport and communications, power and public services that would secure rapid development. Now, that enthusiasm seems to have subsided.

Too much of a reliance on foreign aid, from whatever source, results in a dependency relationship between developed and developing nations with which the latter understandably are ill at ease. Still, only a few developing countries totally (or almost totally) reject foreign resources, since such a rejection would restrict their development options and, other things being equal, their rate of economic growth. But past aid allocation does not seem to be primarily determined by economic considerations. In examining the pattern of aid allocation, one can conclude that aid is not adjusted to the population size of the recipients; it is by no means adjusted to the situation of the beneficiaries; its effectiveness seems to bear no relation to the efforts made; and the political factor explains certain concentrations of resources. Furthermore, no aid or as little as possible is donated to those countries politically, emotionally, or ideologically at odds with the donor. Often, nothing or as little as possible is donated to poor but politically reliable countries. Instead, resources are withheld to be used elsewhere.

It has been further shown that the maximum aid is earmarked for actual or potential allies whose political situation is unstable and where it is hoped that a little economic well-being will restore internal equilibrium and confirm loyalty. Griffin and Enos (1970a:325) have observed that foreign aid tends to strengthen the status quo; it enables those in power to evade and avoid fundamental reforms and it does little more than patch plaster on the deteriorating social edifice.

Obviously, this practice of providing or withholding aid for political reasons considerably weakens its usefulness in advancing development. United States' aid, for example, is not distributed among countries in such a way as to provide a strong incentive for effective self-help measures. Because aid is used for security and political purposes as well as to promote development, the pattern of United States' aid allocations does not favour good performers clearly enough to induce them to maintain their efforts or to encourage other nations to improve on poor past records.

Essentially, what the critics of aid have been saying is that aid is used as an instrument for domesticating the developing countries; that it is seriously ill-conceived, but contains the strategy for maximising United States' and other Western countries' self-interests and that the multilateral agencies have exercised leverage.

The arguments for and against aid and its structure have been many and varied. However, aid seems to be a permanent feature of the process of international resource assistance. The extent to which it is distributed in accordance with the true principles of equity and efficiency reflects the contribution of the well-to-do members of the international community toward eliminating the imbalances and inequalities within the world economic system. But, regardless of its underlying motive, aid has to be scrutinised by the recipients from the totality of their own self-interest.

Aid should be sought and given only if it enhances national economic development, which lessens economic dependence where growth is merely but one aspect, a necessary but not sufficient condition. Indeed, international assistance that is given without regard to the relative needs of the recipients is self-defeating in that its contribution to the development of the recipient country is highly unlikely to be very fruitful. As such, the contributions of the rich economies toward the development requirements of the poor nations should be geared to the development needs of the latter and not to the interests, both political and economic, of the rich countries (Singer and Ansari, 1977:143). Aid should, therefore, be examined by the recipient countries within the context of their long-term strategy for economic development geared to self-reliance and the attainment of economic independence and should not be seen as an instrument of political alignment (Mikesell, 1983:100–2).

In any case, the level and outlook for aid is cause for some serious concern to the low-income countries. Some donor countries have taken the position that economic and budgetary difficulties are adding new limits to their foreign aid programs. In the United States, which already donates the least in terms of the proportion of its GNP, new budget proposals

Table 2.2
Aid Flows from Major Donors, 1970-1979
(Percentage Share)

Donor	1970	1975	1979
DAC Group	86.4	66.7	76.1
Non market Countries	13.6	6.7	6.3
OPEC	0	26.6	17.6

Source: World Bank, World Development Report, 1981
(Washington, D.C.: World Bank, 1981).

indicate that future aid will be lower than had seemed probable a year ago. The United Kingdom has also announced cuts in previously planned programs.

However, the Arab and Scandinavian countries have maintained high ratios of development assistance to GNP, while Japan and Canada have indicated their intent to increase their foreign aid donations.

As can be seen from table 2.2, the development assistance group of countries still continues to contribute the majority of aid. However, OPEC's share has increased dramatically since 1970. The majority of the aid is distributed to the middle-income countries (approximately 39 percent) while the low-income countries receive 19 percent. Aid to the middle-income countries is heavily biased toward three groups of countries. Israel and Egypt, together, receive about 7.2 percent of their GNP and 22 percent of their imports in aid, mostly from the United States. Similarly, OPEC's aid is heavily concentrated on contributions to Jordan and Syria while French aid goes to its overseas territories in the form of technical assistance.

External Borrowing and the Debt Problem of Developing Nations

Borrowing and lending across political borders dates back at least to the ancient civilisations of the Mediterranean and probably much further into the past to tribal societies. However, during the last decade, the external indebtedness of the developing countries has been of growing concern, particularly with respect to the non-oil-developing nations.

As can be seen in table 2.3, the LDCs accumulated substantial amounts of external debt over the past decade, and this indebtedness has expanded considerably with the oil price increases of 1979–1980. The outstanding medium- and long-term debt increased more than sixfold in nominal terms between 1970 and 1980 at an average annual rate of 20.5 percent, reaching $438.7 billion by the end of 1980, compared with only $67.7 billion as recently as 1970. The low-income oil importers' debt grew less rapidly, since they depended more on grants. The single most important factor in these increases was the rapid rate of inflation. In real terms, outstanding debt grew at around 10 percent a year, compared with about 12 percent a year during the 1960s.

However, the growth of the external debt of developing nations cannot be considered in isolation. Rather, it must be viewed in the broader context of the overall external positions of the developing nations and their underlying stability and growth. The fundamental changes that have occurred in recent years in the external environment facing developing nations are reflected in the level and structure of their external indebtedness; the large external imbalance in prospect for many of them will require further reliance on external financing associated with substantial adjustment of efforts.

Table 2.3
Medium- and Long-Term External Debt
Outstanding and Disbursed, 1970-1980

Country Group	Billions of Current Dollars		Billions of 1978 Dollars		Percent Real Growth
	1970	1980	1970	1980	1970-1980
Oil Importers	48.0	301.3	102.6	250.9	9.4
Low Income	(14.5)	(48.0)	(31.0)	(40.0)	2.6
Middle Income	(33.5)	(253.3)	(71.6)	(210.9)	11.4
Oil Exporters	19.7	137.4	42.1	114.4	10.5
All Developing Nations	67.7	438.7	144.7	365.3	9.7

Source: World Bank, World Development Report, 1981 (Washington, D.C.: World Bank, 1981).

Much of the debate on the external debt question now focuses on the issue of debt servicing capacity. The debt service ratio is used to measure the liquidity problem that may arise from fixed debt service obligations. The high rates of growth of debt and debt service since 1970 have been associated with attempts by developing nations to maintain investment and economic growth in the face of an increasingly unstable external environment arising from wide fluctuations of commodity prices and larger current deficits owing to higher import costs. However, the single most important factor in the increase of nominal debt and debt servicing obligations was the more rapid pace of inflation.

The growth of debt was not excessive in relation to GNP or exports as seen in table 2.4. The debt to GNP ratio increased over the 1970s but, measured against exports of goods and services, the debt ratio was lower in 1980 than it had been in 1970. However, significant changes in the composition of debt have increased the burden of servicing it.

During the past decade, there has been a sharp decline in the share of net borrowing from bilateral official sources, a marginal increase in the share coming from multilateral institutions and a large increase in the proportion of loans from private sources, primarily commercial banks. Private financial institutions held 12 percent of outstanding private and publicly guaranteed debt in 1970 compared to 43 percent in 1980.

The growth in commercial borrowing by LDCs has given rise to the Syndicated Eurocurrency Credit Market. Syndicated Eurocredits are loans in which a group of financial institutions make funds available on common conditions to a borrower. They have emerged as a popular vehicle for international lending because they contain advantages from the point of view of both lenders and borrowers. From the lenders' viewpoint, the syndication procedure is a means for banks to diversify some of the unique risks that arise in international lending while at the same time allowing different-sized banks to function in the market simultaneously. From the viewpoint of the LDCs, syndication allows for the efficient arrangement of a larger amount of funds than any single lender

Table 2.4
Indicators of Developing Countries' Outstanding Debt, 1970–1979
(Percentages)

Indicators	1970	1971	1972	1973	1974	1975	1976	1977	1978	1979
Debt Service Ratio	8.9	9.2	9.0	8.8	7.1	8.4	8.4	9.5	12.4	12.6
Interest Service Ratio	2.8	2.9	2.8	2.7	2.4	3.2	3.3	3.5	4.2	4.8
Capital Service Ratio	14.5	14.5	13.4	13.4	11.1	11.9	11.5	12.9	15.5	15.0
Debt/GNP	12.3	13.1	13.5	13.1	12.6	13.9	15.5	17.0	18.3	17.8
Debt/Exports	80.1	85.2	81.8	70.0	59.6	72.1	75.6	79.6	86.6	78.3
Debt/Reserves	263.7	239.9	183.2	153.9	143.5	193.9	204.6	214.5	217.3	176.4
Interest Service/GNP	0.4	0.4	0.5	0.5	0.5	0.6	0.7	0.7	0.9	1.1

Source: World Bank, World Development Report, 1981 (Washington, D.C.: World Bank, 1981).

can feasibly supply. Moreover, it is generally free of restrictions and therefore allows a greater degree of policy independence. Also, it can usually be negotiated fairly rapidly and drawn on without delay to help cope with sudden pressures on a country's balance of payments. Interest on syndicated loans is usually computed by adding a spread to the London interbank offer rate (LIBOR). LIBOR is the rate at which banks lend funds to other banks operating in the Euromarket. The LIBOR changes continuously. However, the rate on any particular loan is readjusted only every three or six months. This is known as pricing on a rollover basis.

The terms on syndicated lending (spreads and maturity of loans) which were easy in 1973 tightened significantly in 1974 when spreads widened and maturities shortened. Thereafter, conditions eased considerably and a "borrowers' market" was created in 1978 and 1979 in which almost all borrowers were able to negotiate fine terms on their syndicated loans. Since the beginning of 1980 the oil-importing LDCs had to face generally stiffer terms, however, combined with high average levels of LIBOR (Fleming, 1981:10).

The large shifts in net financing and net flows reflect not only the speed with which commitments and disbursements were increased but also the marked rise in debt service to the banks. The large increase in the share of bank debt in total debt quickly produced a deterioration in the debt service profile for all these countries. Bank lending carries much shorter maturities and grace periods, as well as higher interest rates, than the official bilateral and multilateral loans that had previously constituted the main source of funds. Part of the amount of interest rates is an inflation premium. But even inflation-corrected interest rates have, in recent years, been higher than in the 1960s and early 1970s. Moreover, while the inflation premium compensates for the erosion in the real value of outstanding debt when combined with the shortening of average maturities it aggravates the debt servicing problems of developing nations. Average maturities fell from 20 years in 1970 to 12.7 years in 1980, although the maturities of loans from official sources remained practically the same at 24 years.

Despite the fact that most developing nations have been able to meet principal and interest payments on their external debt, the spread of international syndicated lending and the increasing tendency for more banks to become involved in lending on a wide geographical basis made debt restructuring necessary for some countries.

The banks generally have been willing to consider the restructuring of principal in arrears, but the existence of large overdue balances has tended to make the negotiations more difficult and the banks less willing to include new money in the restructuring package. Most debt restructuring packages are based on the condition of adoption of a stabilisation program. Repayment of rescheduled debts is normally over seven to ten years.

Proposals for debt restructuring have generally assumed that reorganisations should be carried out within a multilateral framework. Such a framework, by bringing together the debtor country and the official creditors, facilitates the rescheduling task by establishing general principles to guide the renegotiations.

Debt relief is, however, objected to on the grounds that it will adversely affect, either permanently or for lengthy periods, the creditworthiness in the interantional capital market of developing countries, either individually or as a group. This is perhaps doubtful though since many developing countries still do not have effective access to capital markets and are unlikely to be able to do so in the immediate future. Moreover, debt relief takes into consideration the economic needs and potential of the debtor country and, as such, actually helps in improving creditworthiness.

Within the limits of a country's international creditworthiness, foreign debt provides an opportunity to spend more than the national product and to borrow against the future. Judicious use of this opportunity may raise the rate of growth and provide the scope to meet the future burden without undue stress. However, any analysis of developing countries' indebtedness over time is beset by the difficulty of taking account of currency realignments and inflation. Currency realignments as well as the floating of currencies have had complex repercussions on the value of debt outstanding, the cost of debt service, the value of reserves and on trade relations in general. Allowing for an increase in dollar prices of developing countries' exports, the real effect of most currency realignments has been a reduction in the debt outstanding. In addition to and related to the effect of currency realignments, the effect of inflation on indebtedness must be taken into account. To the extent that the inflation rate is not fully reflected in setting the interest rate of a loan, inflation is beneficial to the debtors because they service the debt with money which is worth less than when contracting the debt. The effect of inflation is of course more complicated, depending on how the prices of developing countries' exports and imports are affected, as reflected in their terms of trade. The recent disturbances resulting from higher prices for oil, food and other primary products have added a further dimension to the complications of debt comparisons over time (OECD, 1974:10).

As in other fields of debt analysis, the global picture masks considerable differences among individual countries. The beneficial effect of inflation on their debt service is especially pronounced for those countries whose exports prices have risen sharply so that they need to employ that much less in terms of real resources to generate the foreign exchange required for debt service. On the other hand, this result may be nullified as higher import prices reduce the real value of imported goods (OECD, 1974:10–11).

Finding a means through which debt servicing problems can be avoided is the most important task facing creditor and debtor countries. The avoidance of debt servicing problems under conditions that are consistent with an orderly development process in the less-developed countries is in the interest of both sets of countries. The avoidance of debt servicing problems will require appropriate policies by both debtor and creditor countries. These policies have substantial areas of overlap and a broad measure of understanding and complementarity should be promoted to achieve a fruitful rapprochement with respect to matters on which divergencies may exist.

It must be understood, however, that developing countries bear the responsibility to take all reasonable measures within their means to ensure that debt servicing problems are avoided. However, domestic policies designed to avoid debt servicing problems can only be fully successful in a suitable and favourable external environment characterised by frank cooperation between debtor and credit countries.

Avoiding debt service problems requires, among other things, policies with regard to the mobilisation of domestic savings, which have an important bearing on investment programmes and therefore on rates of growth of output. Policies with regard to the allocation of new investments are of special significance and can in many cases be improved through more efficient use of project evaluation.

Due to the importance of export earnings in determining total foreign exchange availabilities in debtor countries, policies in creditor and debtor countries regarding trade have an important bearing on the capacity of the latter to service debt. In this case, appropriate exchange rate and export promotion policies in debtor countries, including, when necessary, the prompt adjustment of exchange rates, will play an important role in fostering an expansion in export earnings. Also in this regard, over the long term there must be a sustained growth of world trade fueled by import demand in the industrial nations. This is required to provide the developing nations with the foreign exchange for their development and with an expanding base to support their external liabilities. Unless world trade improves, exports of developing nations will not improve sufficiently and crises will become more frequent and repetition may turn sluggishness into a recession (Dhonte, 1979:xiv).

Also of importance is the link between external debt management and other policies. The management of external debt should aim at providing the maximum possible net resource transfer that can be sustained over time, while other policies must provide for a sustainable current account outcome consistent with access to foreign borrowing over the medium term.

However, the positions of the developed nations in the debt problem debate have generally reflected their interest and perspective as creditors. They stress their basic concern for the stability of the international financial system, their general abhorrence of the notions of cancellation or default and their belief in principles of good economic management. Particularly, they also emphasise the need to resolve the debt burden problems with traditional measures. Furthermore, from their point of view, any departures from such orthodox action should be taken only on a case-by-case basis.

But where does this leave the LDCs? The economic burden of external debt is simply the giving up of real resources as interest and amortisation payments are made. For the debt burden to remain manageable, the industrial nations must make loan concessions to the LDCs. This burden should remain manageable as long as the addition to output made possible by a loan exceeds the claim on resources as debt service payments are made. So long as borrowers receive more in new loans than they must pay out for debt servicing, the economic burden may not seem pressing. Unless external borrowing makes a net contribution, that is, unless its economic benefits exceed its costs, external debt will tend to rise much faster than gross domestic product and borrowing to pay for interest and amortisation on the debt will also accelerate, which can lead to a potentially dangerous situation.

3

The Concept of Development Administration

Development administration, or the public administration of economic development, has gained rapid recognition in recent years and has resulted in a growing amount of literature being published on it. Primarily, it applies to the activities of governments to achieve development or modernisation. To be most useful, development administration can be applied not only to goal-oriented, change-minded administration but also to those countries that have as a top priority the change from low productivity to much higher productivity levels sustained over a reasonably long period of time. The level of economic productivity in which the public administrator operates is the essence of the need for distinguishing among other types of public administration and development administration.

The administration of development in developing countries is effected primarily through politicians and the civil service operating within a ministerial system or government agency and is characterised by its purposes, its loyalties and its attitudes. The purposes of development administration are to stimulate and facilitate defined programmes of social and economic progress or, put another way, development administration is the administration of policies, programmes and projects to serve development purposes. It is the term used to denote the complex of agencies, management systems and processes a government establishes to achieve its development goals. It thus encompasses the organisation of new agencies such as planning organisations and development corporations, the reorientation of established agencies such as departments of agriculture, the delegation of administrative powers to development agencies and the creation of a cadre of administrators who can provide leadership in stimulating and supporting programmes of social and economic improvement (Gant, 1966:200; Anstee, 1981:48–53). Development administration, like development planning in the LDCs, is mainly a postwar phenomenon. It emerged both as a discipline and a process through which government programmes for economic development were implemented and administered in the hope of achieving the best possible results or maximum social gain for society.

Significant attempts have been made at achieving a simple working definition of the term *development administration*, which is still referred to in some publications as "comparative public administration." Development administration from a conceptual point of view is, for the most part, a by-product of the comparative study of public administration in developing countries. However, the substance of development administration is quite solid and tangible.

Merle Fainsod (1963:2) emphasised the innovating thrust of development administration. In his theoretical approach he stated:

Development administration is a carrier of innovating values. As the term is commonly used, it embraces the array of new functions assumed by developing countries embarking on the path of modernisation and industrialisation. Development administration ordinarily involves the establishment of machinery for planning economic growth and mobilising and allocating resources to expand national income. New administrative units, frequently called nation-building departments, are set up to foster industrial development, manage new state economic enterprises, raise agricultural output, develop natural resources, improve the transportation and communication network, reform the educational system, and achieve other developmental goals.

Fred Riggs's (1971:73) approach to a definitional framework was to point out that there was an essential difference between the administration of development and development of administration—two different but interrelated aspects of development administration. His definition couched in simple short-run terms was as follows:

Development administration refers to organised efforts to carry out programs or projects thought by those involved to serve developmental objectives.

The phrase (development administration) arises by simple analogy, with such expressions as agricultural administration, educational administration, and social welfare administration, each of which involves organised efforts to implement agricultural, educational, and social welfare programs, respectively.

He noted further that development administration refers not only to a government's efforts to carry out programmes designed to reshape its physical, human and cultural environment, but also to the struggle to enlarge a government's capacity to engage in such programmes.

More recent studies have examined development administration both from a conceptual and an operational point of view. Jean-Claude Garcia-Zamor (1973:422), for example, writes:

Development administration in this context is the bureaucratic process that facilitates or stimulates the achievement of socio-economic progress through the utilisation of the talents and expertise of the bureaucrats. It involves the mobilisation of bureaucratic skills for speeding up the development process.

It seems distinctly clear from the foregoing definitions that development administration in contextual and operational terms implies efficient organisation and management of the development activities of a nation to attain the goals of development. It is also the process of guiding an organisation toward the achievement of progressive political, economic and social objectives that are authoritatively determined as agents and subjects of change (Timsit, 1981:71–83). It is the conscious study of the conditions of public administration in the less-developed countries. It is the study of what is expected of public administration in the LDCs (Swerdlow, 1975:347; Dwivedi and Nef, 1982:59–77).

Since 1962, there has been a significant change in attempts to study development administration. The change has been from normative approaches to empirical approaches to regressive approaches. Some of the empirical work was done by Ferrel Heady (1966), who sought to compare higher civil bureaucracies in a variety of existing political systems. Riggs (1964), on the other hand, had developed what he termed "the theory of prismatic society." By a gross ill-fitting analogy with the prism which is interposed between "fused" white light and the "diffracted" rainbow of all the colours, he named the intermediate society "prismatic"—halfway between fused or undifferentiated societies and diffracted or modern societies with high internal specialisation. In prismatic societies, people hold two ideals at once, switching from the traditional set of behaviors to the modern without apparent embarrassment or confusion. Conflict between the two is not often articulated, but is recognised by the acceptance of an endemic gap between formal expectations and actual behaviour.

Other studies have attempted to examine development administration in terms of its temporal dimensions, its spatial dimensions, and even through critical path analysis. Dwight Waldo (1970) edited the study on temporal dimensions of development administration. His primary conclusions were: (1) differing, culturally given perceptions of the temporal factor (time) are extremely important in administration and development, and (2) the temporal dimension is extremely important in large-scale efforts in the transfer of administrative technologies and in large-scale administrative reforms.

The existing study on spatial dimensions of development administration, which appeared as a companion volume to the study on temporal dimensions, was edited by James Heaphey (1971). The study appears to be less conclusive than the one on temporal aspects, and not surprisingly so, since one can make a solid argument that a society oriented toward space is a static society, whereas a society oriented toward progressive time is a dynamic society.

The major work on critical path analysis for development administration was done by Packard (1972). *Critical path* means those activities that, taken together, determine the shortest overall possible time of the project. This assumes, of course, that a determination has been made of the event and activity times for a project with the result that it can be distinguished between the various activities of the project. There are significant weaknesses in critical path analysis, however, when applied to development administration. The primary weakness stems from the fact that there is imprecise notion of project time. Moreover, great difficulty could be encountered in attempting to define efficient objectives.

The work on regressive development administration was developed by Quah (1979) who argued that the concept of development administration has a unilinear bias and does not take into account the possibility of failure. It is that possibility of failure that gives rise to the concept of regressive administration. Regressive administration refers to a situation in which development administration does not result from a government's attempt at administrative reform, and one in which the organisations undergoing reform are unable to attain their goals. As such, Quah (1979:32) believes, and agreeably so, that "development administration refers to the administration of developmental programmes designed to promote nation-building and socio-economic development and the concomitant development of administrative practices and institutions necessary for the implementation of such programmes."

THE STRUCTURE OF DEVELOPMENT ADMINISTRATION IN DEVELOPING NATIONS

Development administration in the less-developed countries was shaped primarily by the colonial overlords during their period of rule, and although after achieving independence there has been some attempt at reorganising, changing, reforming and improving the entire administrative structure to function effectively in the service of independent nations, development administration in the LDCs still remains a product of the colonial era, maintaining many of the features and attitudes of the former colonial establishments.

The structure of development administration in the LDCs has, however, evolved through a number of phases to its present form based on a system of agencies that are, for the most part, called ministries. During the colonial era the day-to-day administration of development was carried out through various departments and each of these was administered by a chief professional officer who was, in turn, responsible to a colonial secretary or governor as the case may be. The colonial secretaries or governors were responsible for overall administrative functions and they were in turn accountable only to their imperial governments or monarchies and were primarily concerned with their future careers than with the business of administration for development.

Within that framework, local-born members of the civil service were forced to accept positions to perform routine clerical functions. Local public opinion was disregarded and the societies drifted more and more into one of class structures. Because the centralised colonial state bureaucracy exercised political power and was also directly responsible for the management of the economy on behalf of imperial interests, its dominance over the social system was literally all-embracing and it used its vast resources to sponsor dependent classes that were committed to the maintenance of the status quo (Jones and Mills, 1976:326). It can be summarised, therefore, that in terms of problem solving, the patterns of administrative institutionalisation during the colonial era have been noninnovative and were created and organised not so much to promote development and indigenous problem-solving techniques, but rather to harmonise and consolidate elite interests, especially with respect to the kinds of problems that were to be recognised and solved.

With the achievement of internal self-government and political independence, decision making and executive authority in the LDCs were transferred from the colonial governors and secretaries to local politicians and their cabinets. This resulted in the creation of a ministerial system of administration. This new system gave native elected officials the general direction and control of their respective governments and they were collectively responsible to their respective legislatures.

With the creation of the ministerial system in the LDCs, there was a shift of the locus of responsibility for policy formation from a chief professional officer to a minister of an elected government. Each ministry is usually staffed with a principal adviser to the minister as well as several other advisers responsible for various areas of policymaking regarded as necessary.

Some developing countries have attempted to follow the British model of public administration. This model is one in which the civil service is not politically controlled. Here the situation is simply one in which the administrators are not servants of the person who is the Head of State or servants of any other person or groups of persons but servants of the public or the people. This model of public administration was established by the British in the middle of the nineteenth century and it was part of an effort to weaken the power of the King and to strengthen that of Parliament through a system that would ensure that public administrators would change their position from that of servants of the King to that of servants of the people. Civil servants as such became nonpartisan. It was Parliament, as the body representing the people, that enacted the laws. The public administrators only implemented the laws and carried out the policies, and they were expected to do so in a businesslike and efficient manner.

This approach toward public administration, or development administration in the case of the LDCs, is regarded as the orthodox theory. The orthodox theory emphasises the instrumental nature of administration. The legal duties of the civil service are confined to the implementation of policies. It accepts the concept of political neutrality as a salient feature of modern public administrative techniques.

The orthodox theory is one of formal organisation based on a unified and disciplined system of authority. Such a system represents a joint or collective effort for achieving specified objectives. This model of organisation is a meritocracy. The civil servant is selected or recruited on the basis of merit and guaranteed a career in the service with career development and promotion based on his or her performance and seniority. The orthodox theory is therefore based on the principle of a clear line of authority defining superior-inferior relationships or a pattern of hierarchy.

PROBLEMS OF ADMINISTERING
DEVELOPMENT IN DEVELOPING NATIONS

The administration of development in the LDCs has always had some serious drawbacks, both during and after colonial rule. Despite serious attempts after independence to restructure the system of development administration and to increase its effectiveness and impact, there still exists a number of factors, primarily a legacy of the colonial past, that impede the process. The fundamental factors responsible for the situation are as follows.

First, there is a general lack of high-level manpower necessary for policy implementation. Here we are referring particularly to the scarcity of trained administrators. No lasting and significant process of growth and development can be achieved in the economy of any developing nation unless there are sufficient human skills and resources present there that can be used to implement and thereby assist in prolonging the development cycle (Rondinelli, 1976:10–11). The lack of trained administrators in the LDCs is the direct result of three factors: (1) chronic "brain drain," (2) poor government recruitment policies, and (3) lack of proper manpower planning and assessment.

The first two factors were brought about, ultimately, from the third. The lack of proper manpower planning and assessment produced haphazard recruitment policies, underemployment and unemployment, and, inevitably, frustration on the part of the few skilled administrators present that forced them to emigrate.

Development planning in the LDCs has been myopic in its basically nonoccupation with the human factor and its preoccupation with economic factors. One gets the impression that the planners regarded the development plans as self-implementing. But development entails more than economic factors and measures. It requires a far broader strategy and more comprehensive administrative initiatives than now prevail. Development in this context is relative and involves value judgments and tasks beyond those reflected in economic indicators. The priceless asset of any country is its human resource. As such, great emphasis must be placed on a society's perception of human life—to man's intellectual and spiritual potential (Stone and Stone, 1976:196). Without any significant attempt on the part of the governments of LDCs to plan manpower within the framework of development plans, development plan implementation will be anything but successful.

Currently in the LDCs there exists a highly bureaucratic civil service and excessive centralisation of authority and control. This excessive centralisation is reflected in government ministers assuming total control of their respective ministries and departments in terms of decision making and paying inadequate attention to or giving little opportunity to middle- or lower-level civil servants to participate in the decision-making process or in the development process. This situation continues to be perpetrated because the civil service in most LDCs has become an institution in which personnel survival, in terms of longevity of service, depends on political affiliation—a situation that does not conform to the regulations governing the usually nonpolitical nature of the civil service.

Moreover, there exists a great deal of friction, tension and mutual suspicion between government ministers and career officials. Both the ministers and the career officials have adopted an attitude toward the implementation of policy that has alienated the public and hampered the effective functioning of the government. Career civil servants are in a position of great insecurity due to the enormous powers of the government ministers. Most of the career civil servants, if not all of them, are usually better educated than the ministers (who are appointed primarily on the basis of their politics), and find it difficult to abide by the decisions of the ministers, whom they regard as inadequately educated and not competent enough to make decisions pertaining to the administration of development. The ministers, on the other hand, conscious of

their newly acquired powers and determined to dispel any
suggestion of inferiority, are anxious to assert their authority
and to make it clear beyond doubt who are the masters (United
Nations, 1982:49–50). Inevitably then, for reasons of survival
within the civil service, career civil servants have to adopt a
sycophantic and fanatical attitude toward their ministers; of-
fering technical and administrative advice to these ministers
not in a firm and objective manner but by attempting to anticipate the advice the minister wants.

The ultimate result of all of these manifestations is a lack
of coordination of policies among departments and a lack of
dissemination of information for effective decision making.
Invariably then, the few individuals at the apex of the decision-making pyramid, namely the ministers, are hard pressed
to cope with the range of decisions they have to make. The
effect is necessarily either procrastination and long delays or
inadequate and inept policies.

It is clear that the centralised nature of the civil service in
LDCs contributes to the destruction of the channels of communication in the organisation and tends to immobilise development administration. After independence in the LDCs
then, the bureaucratic, colonial-oriented administration was
transformed into a bureaucratic organisation that emphasised
the sovereignty of politics rather than the supremacy of administration (Hope, 1977a:69). Politics became the most important activity and the politician (minister) came to occupy
a position of unquestionable supremacy in matters of decision making (Dube, 1964:233; United Nations, 1982:49–50).

Of major significance among the factors affecting the administration of development in LDCs is the lack of the political leadership's total support for the improvement of the nation's administrative system. Administrative change inevitably
involves a challenge to accepted modes of action and traditional values and perogatives (Chikulo, 1981:56–57). Projects
for administrative reform, if they are other than routine and
minor, must be backed fully by the chief executive of the nation and his or her cabinet. In speaking of the vital importance of leadership here, we are alluding to the critical place
of authority in national development. If political leaders are

to inspire a population and to direct the bureaucracy to higher levels of performance and development, their words and actions must carry an aura of legitimacy. Historically, political leaders in the LDCs have been primarily concerned with maintaining their own existence as politicians and this has resulted in much confusion between the administrative and political function in the decision-making process and in the creation of political elites, who alone cannot execute the services and achieve developmental goals.

Functional reform of development administration, as needed in LDCs, can only be brought about through a derived effort and the critical support of the political leadership. Constitutional changes and the pressures for development have brought about the need for new attitudes toward administrative reform on the part of the government. Any continued lack of support by the government will inevitably continue to perpetrate and legitimise an inefficient and irresponsive bureaucracy. A bureaucracy the LDCs cannot afford to have if the primary emphasis is on the promotion of growth, development, equity and provision of basic-needs for a once-colonised people.

To add to the difficulty, government functions in LDCs are generally dispersed among an excessive number of ministers, authorities and agencies. Since independence, new agencies, public corporations and ministries to fulfill development objectives have been superimposed without a prior review of the entire structure. The inevitable result is a multiplicity of organs, duplication of function and diffusion of responsibility. For example, in Guyana there is currently in existence a Timber Export Board, a Timbers Corporation and a Forest Industries Corporation, all of which have responsibility for wood products. Surely, one public corporation could have been created and charged with the responsibility for all forest and timber products (Hope, 1979b:200).

Along with the proliferation of public and quasi-public enterprises has been the attempt by the governments of LDCs to administer these enterprises on the basis of traditional governmental control or, conversely, for a few enterprises to provide such a degree of autonomy that the institutions are no longer accountable to the public interest. The rationale for the establishment of public corporations in LDCs stems primarily from the same reasons that development planning has become a vigorous activity and from the attempt of governments to provide basic needs without the masses being exploited. The establishment of public and quasi-public enterprises were seen, therefore, as a necessary ingredient in the development process. Public and quasi-public enterprises emerged in LDCs because recognition was given to the fact that the private sector lacked the urge and the ability to ensure growth, efficiency and equity (Ahmad, 1982:49–64). The maximisation of efficiency and output (the achievement of Pareto optimum) by the private sector depends upon a host of restrictive conditions: perfect competition must prevail in all product and factor markets; correct information about present and future price and nonprice variables must be available. Consumers' tastes must be given and be independent of each other; producers must attempt to maximise profits. Capital must be divisible; there must be no increasing returns to scale, otherwise competition will break down; and external economies must be absent. Even supposing these conditions existed, it does not follow that an unregulated economy, in terms of the price system, would be ideal for the LDCs.

In the first place, the role of the private sector within the framework of the market mechanism is to foster efficiency, not equity. There is no suggestion that the distribution of income under a Pareto optimum is ideal or even acceptable. The sole implication of the optimum is that more of one commodity can be obtained only by having less of another and one individual can be made better off only by making someone else worse off. This, however, does not enable us to compare the welfare implications of one Pareto optimum with another or even to compare a point of maximum efficiency with many nonoptimum positions. Once the distribution of income is admitted to be a variable, it is no longer true that if one person is "better off" and none "worse off" the welfare of the nation is increased; national welfare may, indeed, decline. There can be no impartial assessment; it all depends on value judgments.

Moreover, the private sector and the price system is concerned with static resource allocation, not growth. The most that theory demonstrates is that an efficiently functioning market economy will maximise current output from its given factor endowments. This tells us nothing about the rate at which capital is accumulated, the speed with which the quality of the labour force is improved or the pace of exploration and discovery of natural resources. One cannot automatically assume that static efficiency will be associated with rapid growth. In fact, it has been demonstrated that both "static" and "dynamic" efficiency are lower in the Soviet Union than in the United States, yet the Soviet Union was able to achieve a high rate of capital accumulation and build a modern industrial economy in less than forty years on a foundation established prior to 1917. No capitalist or free enterprise economy—including Japan and the United States—has ever approached that record (Griffin and Enos, 1970b:23).

The foregoing substantively represents the thinking of the economic advisers of the governments of LDCs vis-à-vis the need for public corporations. Undoubtedly, these views make sound economic sense and a significant amount of literature supporting those points of view has emerged in recent years. Malcolm Gillis (1980), for instance, has argued that whatever the ultimate perspective may be, the country anxious to develop economically has no alternative but to use public enterprise on a considerable scale, at the very least, to get things going. How much is left to private initiative will depend partly on ideology but to a much greater extent on social and economic circumstances. Yet, others have argued for the creation of public enterprise to promote those social objectives not readily consistent with profit maximisation in the private sector (Sheahan, 1976:205–30). But, alas, irrespective of the reasons in favour of the creation of public enterprise, there still remains the issue of accountability of these enterprises in the LDCs. There currently exists too much political control of public enterprise in LDCs. Undoubtedly, there is a dilemma created in terms of autonomy versus control. For public enterprises, achieving accountability is complicated by the need to permit sufficient freedom for the enterprise to operate (Howard, 1982).

The trend toward governmental planning further complicates the picture. Against the traditional right of an enterprise to manage its own affairs, there is posed the right of government, under planning, to use all of its resources in the best way possible. The contrasts in the situation before and after planning can be overemphasised. Many authors on public enterprise would maintain that governments have always had the duty to prevent enterprises from becoming isolated islands unresponsive to governmental wishes. The issue has been prominent in discussing the future of public enterprise in developing areas. The right of governments to use public enterprise within the overall planning effort to promote growth is both necessary and accepted. Public enterprise in LDCs comprises a significant part of the public sector and inevitably would be figured into the development plans. What tends to remain, however, are public enterprises that are political in outlook and that lack accountability to the populace.

Another factor affecting development administration in the LDCs is that of the level of economic development. The degree of economic development and the state of development administration are closely linked. Reasonably good development administration is one of the conditions for economic development; at the same time, the level of economic development influences the level of administration (Paul, 1983:21–42). In the LDCs, the level of economic development is hampered particularly by low growth of agriculture, weak balance-of-payments performance and persistent high unemployment.

At low levels of economic development, the demand for efficiency of government agencies is less urgent. The rhythm of life is slower and things move in set patterns. There is little difference between the ways of administration and the ways of life beyond the office (Dabasi-Schweng, 1965:21). On the other hand, higher levels of economic development create demands on the efficiency of government agencies while at the same time they provide the input to allow the agencies to cope with increasingly complex and technical tasks. Administrative systems tend to grow to cope with the developing needs of a modern society and the process of expansion that results. Speed and flexibility become essential factors in the efficiency of development administration.

A development administration that lags behind is a brake on economic development, while a development administration that is too far advanced will jeopardise the process instead of promoting it. Obviously, development administration has to exert leadership and has to be ahead of the community, but it cannot be too far ahead. Otherwise, a situation will develop similar to that known to engineers when a centrifugal pump is used to lift water to a higher level than that for which it was constructed. The water column will break and no water will be lifted at all.

There are three levels at which the interrelationship between the administrative processes and economic development need to be examined and appraised: (1) technology, (2) techniques or procedures, and (3) forms or organisations (Swerdlow, 1975:77).

In technology, the impact of economic development on public administration processes is great. In certain fields the use of the technologies taken over from the advanced countries is inevitable; the LDCs cannot be expected to develop these technologies, and there is no need for them to do so. Advanced technology is not restricted to fields like public health, to laboratories testing materials procured by public agencies and so on. Electronic data processing is now used by LDCs to a degree that is truly surprising. In addition, advanced technology seems to involve higher quantities of production based on the nature of technology. The more specialised equipment is worthwhile if it contributes to increments of output. Illustrations of these situations abound. A factory that uses an automatic stamping machine will need to produce far more articles than one that uses a hand-operated stamping machine. Higher production and productivity are the basic reason for specialised equipment, and that such equipment is generally associated with a large volume of output at a lower unit price is not surprising. It is also true that specific technologies come in lumps; that is, there is a finite number of ways to produce a product and each will be related to an optimum output. Consequently, what economists call economies of scale are really a manifestation of technology and are a fact of life for the less-developed countries (Swerdlow, 1975:77).

In the case of techniques or procedures, the impact is also great. Much is taken over, like supervised credit and extension service in agriculture. But the results are not always as happy as in the case of technology. In the case of the machine, given a proper level of maintenance, which is often guaranteed by the makers, the successful operation of the machine is not so completely dependent on the human agent as is the case with procedures. With procedures, the human agent does the job. Because of this, procedures are not as transferable as they would seem at first glance.

At the organisational level, many forms are instituted, but often they do not thrive well. Schools and industrial plants have many similarities in their organisational structure, their need for support and their relationships to the people and organisations that use their products. They also have many important differences. The educational system cannot be operated in the same manner as the banking system, yet in their operations they may have to appraise many problems and examine many influential forces in substantially the same manner. Thus, it is possible to examine the process of organisation using many of the same variables that have been identified as useful in the analysis of other kinds of institutions.

The administration of development in LDCs has also been hampered by the failure of the public to realise what can be achieved by community effort. In many cases, considerable potential awaits development but no action is taken by the people because they do not understand the opportunities that exist, they lack confidence to venture into new activities and their traditional leaders frequently fail to see that they have any function to guide and inspire their people in these matters.

Particularly in the immediate postindependence era, great possibilities existed to channel a powerful stream of human energy and goodwill into constructive projects. Through a process of education, using community development techniques, people can gain the knowledge and confidence required to bring about various kinds of social and economic development. Some areas in which public education is needed include cooperative training and the functions of local government. The traditional leaders can come to appreciate their new role in local and national progress in a similar way.

In every society, some traditional social attitudes militate against development (for example, excessive individualism), while others provide a positive or stabilising force (for example, attachment to land). Community development workers can lead the people to identify their problems, to view them constructively in the light of selected traditional values, and to work together for a more satisfactory life.

One final point to be made, with respect to administrative obstacles to development in LDCs, is that there is insufficient cooperation at the regional level between authorities in the central governments and authorities in the local governments. Unproductive relationships exist and have resulted in a hampering of the implementation of development projects. This obstacle occurs primarily because there may be differences in perspective with respect to national policies. For historical reasons, present district and other boundaries are in many cases related to ethnic groupings or other matters and not to population distribution and economic activity.

MEASURES FOR THE IMPROVEMENT OF DEVELOPMENT ADMINISTRATION IN DEVELOPING NATIONS

From the foregoing discussion, it is obvious that in the LDCs administrative reforms are necessary so as to make administration a fit instrument for carrying out social and economic policies and achieving socioeconomic goals of development. The administrative changes that are necessary must be different from the conventional organisational reforms. Thus, Western concepts applied in the interest of development administration cannot be introduced into the administrative system in LDCs. Hence, all of the remaining attitudes, features and characteristics of the colonial civil service need to be urgently eradicated through processes of reeducation and reorientation to bring the native civil servants in line with the current development thrust.

This brings us then to stressing the point of the crucial importance of increasing administrative capability or operational effectiveness of the LDCs' civil service if development is to be accelerated there. Unless there is a primary and continuing focus on creating administrative capability throughout each nation, there will inevitably be poor performance in formulating programmes and budgets, mobilising resources, recruiting and developing staff, fostering supportive cultural adaptations, building and operating physical and social infrastructure and the daily tasks of managing programmes, projects and services.

One way of fostering administrative capability is to organise major administrative reform programmes. These are defined as specially designed efforts to induce fundamental changes in public administration through system-wide transformation or at least through measures for improvement of one or more of its key elements, such as administrative structure, territorial organisation, budget management, planning process, personnel practices and other administrative processes in response to significant changes, actual or anticipated, in the environment and role of public administration.

A large number of developing countries organised programmes of major administrative reform in the past but did not always clearly stipulate the specific objectives to be achieved through such programmes or spell out the time frames for various actions. Consequently, in such cases the reform programmes had only limited effect on public administration for development. For that reason, the objectives of any administrative reform programme in LDCs should be properly enunciated to provide, at least, the basis for evaluation of results.

To ensure effectiveness of major administrative reform programmes, it is also necessary to pay special attention to their preparation and implementation phases. To the extent possible, it is desirable to involve all concerned in the reform process and to minimise uncertainties, tensions and resistance among affected organisations and functionaries, which are frequently found to accompany major changes. The implementation of reforms should also include training and briefing in new measures, provisions for feedback and corrective action and assistance in installing new systems and methods.

A related approach to reforming public administration for development in the LDCs is to relate pertinent measures directly to national plan objectives, strategies, sectors and programmes in the plan itself. Described as "administrative planning," it calls for spelling out and providing for specific administrative requirements for implementing development plans concurrently with preparation of their economic, social and technical analyses and components. Administrative planning to develop implementing organisations and systems is indispensable to any comprehensive development effort. Attention should therefore be drawn to the importance of measures to increase administrative capability for economic and social development, the desirability of making such measures an integral part of development plans at all levels, as appropriate, and the need for such measures to be adequate to enable governments to achieve their goals.

The reform and improvement of administrative systems need to have well-defined objectives, a clear-cut strategy of implementation and sustained follow-up measures. The government of a country would have to decide whether there is a need for comprehensive reform of the administrative system or whether only incremental improvements would be sufficient for the time being to meet the new needs. However, a tentative generalisation can be made that most developing nations, whether emerging from the colonial rule or otherwise, need periodic comprehensive reform of their respective administrative systems. But while administrative reforms need to be undertaken only periodically, administrative improvements of an incremental type can be undertaken continuously in one field of the administrative system or another. Thus, both basic reform brought about by a comprehensive approach to major administrative problems and the partial approach to specific administrative improvements and innovations have an important role to play.

Administrative reform is political rather than merely organisational. It is a political process designed to adjust the relationship between a bureaucracy and other elements in society or within the bureaucracy itself. It has a moral content in that it seeks to create a better system by removing faults and imperfections. It is usually undertaken to change the status quo for the better and aims at making the administrative and political structures and procedures compatible with broader political goals. The crux of administrative reform, therefore, is innovation; that is, injection of new ideas and new people in a new combination of tasks and relationships into the policy and administrative process. Now let us focus our attention on some more specific measures for creating administrative capability and improving the administration of development in the LDCs.

Manpower Planning and Training

First, there exists an absolute necessity for manpower training in the LDCs. Apart from removing the continued existence of the colonial mentality, education and training are necessary to create a stock of trained administrators. This means an attempt at proper manpower planning and assessment. Manpower planning and assessment go far beyond tabulation of supply and demand indices of the labour force. It must take into consideration the broad spectrum of problems of human resources development. Planning and assessment of manpower should be a part of the development plan of any developing country and should be coordinated with education planning and training. In the LDCs, manpower planning is of vital necessity, but has always been a shortcoming of postindependence development planning in those economies. This shortcoming manifests itself in the negligence or unconcern of the governments and, to a lesser degree, in the lack of qualitative and quantitative techniques necessary for such planning.

Manpower planning is needed in LDCs to ensure the adequate supply of manpower for public organisations that would meet quantitative, qualitative and time requirements of national development plans and programmes. It is therefore necessary to anticipate changes in manpower and skill requirements likely to occur as a result of national development plans and to initiate timely actions to meet them. Manpower planning, as part of the broader planning process, is a useful tool in this respect to deal with the problem in a systematic rather than haphazard manner. It will also provide the basis for planning educational and training activities at various levels. In the LDCs, manpower planning could at least be started for the public sector and be eventually extended to include other sectors of the socioeconomic system.

All developing countries that are facing the challenge of accelerating economic and social development with the consequent responsibility for providing the necessary human and material infrastructure depend critically on the capability, motivation and performance of the personnel in the public services. It is important to recognise the government work force as an indispensable element in national development and, irrespective of the system of recruitment of these public servants, there is a need to improve their capability through training. By training, we mean the act or process of making a person fit to perform certain tasks. Training is necessary because no matter how well qualified a person may be at the time of recruitment, he or she still has certain inadequacies and therefore much to learn before becoming a really effective civil servant. This is the reason why in some countries a person who is newly recruited into the civil service must first go through a period of training before being assigned to specific duties. In France and in countries governed in the French tradition, for example, public administrators must go through a period of training in a national school of administration before joining the various services of the central government. This type of preentry training can be easily undertaken in the LDCs.

Equally important is in-service training. In many countries, national institutes of public administration have been established, for the most part, to provide in-service training at the lower-management and middle-management levels. This may entail a short orientation course of a few days to acquaint a new recruit with his organisation, its environment and the general nature and conditions of work; it may entail some in-

duction training to teach specific tasks and may last a few
weeks; or it may involve a more general training programme
to enhance the administrative capability of a new recruit and
may last for any length of time. In view of the urgency of the work of national development, however, the traditional method of on-the-job training
is often too slow. Sometimes learning by doing or by trial and
error is not only slow but also costly. A formal training programme often speeds up the learning process and thus brings
the civil servants, including new recruits, to a better standard
of performance. The economy of this matter is one of the reasons why formal training has become important in development administration and should be one of its key features. It
should be recognised, though, that some form of tutelage and
on-the-job training is indispensable in the civil services and
that self-development and learning from experience and mistakes have their place. But a formal training programme can
be used to shorten the time required for a person to learn, to
help avoid some of the costly errors of the trial and error
method and at the same time maintain a degree of uniformity
in the substance of training.

Another critical factor in the effectiveness of in-service
training programmes pertains to their substantive content
(Muhammad, 1974:90–100). In-service training by its very
nature tends to be very general and invariably not geared to
any specialised career development. The result is a civil service plagued with dilettantism, immobilism and antiintellec-
tualism. To make in-service training productive, measures must
be undertaken that would meaningfully relate training to the
career development of individual civil servants, to the processes of recruitment, posting, promotion and other terms and
conditions of service such as probationary periods and ex-
aminations. In-service training is not carried out in a vacuum.
It functions in an environment of policies, procedures, standards and institutional objectives and has intimate relationships to other strategies of management.

It is important to make a sharp distinction between the
mere availability of training programmes and their effectiveness in promoting development objectives. Formal training pro-

grammes in many countries, both preentry and postentry, are excessively theoretical and frequently of little operational value. Some are traditional and not development oriented. Some are only for system maintenance and are not change oriented. Some are borrowed without modification from highly developed countries and are irrelevant to the national environment. There is a strong tendency to duplicate university courses in North America or Western Europe rather than to shape courses to meet carefully defined training requirements of the government concerned. Such mistakes must be avoided.

A development administrator today must be a person of intelligence and character, a child of his or her national culture, a person with good intuitive judgment and at the same time a person with a rational approach, a person with an open mind and broad vision, one who shows concern for society as a whole, has a good sense of justice and is well informed and aware of the political implications and social consequences of his or her actions and judgments. Such a person must also identify his or her objectives with the overall development objectives of the nation. In other words, he or she must be development oriented.

Training of civil servants or development administrators must be conceived in very broad terms. It is important to bear in mind that education and training in public administration are long-term processes. No single programme of education or training is able to cover all areas. Some must learn in educational institutions, some in formal training programmes, some through apprenticeship and self-development. A public administrator must continuously learn and improve his or her administrative capability throughout his or her career. In a sense, the whole career is a learning process.

Training and education will, undoubtedly, increase the quality of development administrators, both politicians and career civil servants. Since the quality of development administration and public decision making depends largely on the quality of the policy makers (Armstrong, 1980:185–206), then education and training will directly increase the quality of development administration in the LDCs.

Recognising the basic differences between developed and less-developed countries one can argue that in the development administration training programmes for students from the LDCs three basic orientations are necessary. There is need for a different kind and form of knowledge for promoting creative abilities and innovational attitudes and for promoting motivation and commitment for change. A different kind of knowledge is needed if the knowledge imparted to the students is to be relevant and thus functional. Moreover, relevance of the knowledge gained promotes interest and enthusiasm. The need for developing a sense of creativity and an innovative attitude arises from the fact that some students will have to reconstruct the theories they learned abroad to adapt them to the situation in their own countries. They need to be innovative to successfully accommodate the continually growing and changing interests and demands. The need for promoting motivation and commitment stems from the fact that the rate of development will largely depend upon the enthusiasm of this bureaucratic elite as they will operate, for the most part, in a power vacuum, and most of the initiative for developmental efforts must come either from this elite or it will not materialise at all (Heper, 1975:167).

Decentralisation and Communication

Development administration has been consistently plagued with the tendency toward excessive centralisation. As mentioned earlier, the problem is expressed in the reluctance of government ministers and their permanent secretaries to delegate authority. Insecurity seems to be the major motivating force, and centralised authority is maintained under the banner of political sovereignty and unquestionable supremacy. What seems not to be understood is that this phenomenon creates lags in the administration of development, and attempts should be made at attaining and maintaining a proper balance between the contributions to the quality of decision making by the various units participating in that process.

Undoubtedly, excessive centralisation will be a long-standing phenomenon in the LDCs given the political nature of things. Civil servants currently carry out the decisions made by politicians, thus rejecting their own professional duty to advise. They cling to the privileges and security of their positions without making a serious attempt to contribute to the quality of public policy. What is needed primarily is a role definition of the political part of civil servants in the administration of development and not in national politics as has been advocated. With that reference point, civil servants will have reason to be secure and assert themselves in the process of administering development.

Decentralising the administrative machinery would also serve to improve communication channels and the level of coordination within and among various departments. The dissemination of data and information is vital to a successful development effort. Improved coordination would tend to remove time-consuming, energy-wasting and patience-exhausting checks and counterchecks, references and cross-references, conferences and consultations, often at the wrong levels and about unimportant matters. Effective coordination and communication is crucial to development since it is the only means by which there can be effective control. Moreover, the dynamic management of change depends for its effectiveness on the maintenance of a comprehensive flow of communications through the medium of the public service to the client society (United Nations, 1981:3).

Administrative decentralisation promotes participation, access and responsiveness. Through administrative decentralisation it is possible to emphasise national standards to deal with problems that are national in scope, while at the same time to allow for adjustments to meet particular regional needs. The expertise of professionals is promoted through a vertical integration of the agencies and bureaus of the national government. It is generally agreed that administrative decentralisation should have some place in all systems of modern government. By applying that concept to the structure of government administration, the central government can be "decongested," so that its top administrators are freed from onerous and minor detailed administration and unnecessary involvement in local affairs. As a result, the national government can devote more energy and time to national problems and at the same time facilitate and expedite action on the lower levels. Furthermore, greater civic participation in self-government and feeling for national unity are stimulated (Rondinelli, 1981:133–45) and this will bring about an increase in the people's understanding and support of social and economic development activities and, as a result, gain the benefit of their own contributions to these activities and of personal and group adjustments to needed changes.

Decentralisation should extend both to the lower units in the central hierarchy and to units at the lower levels of government, especially local governments. The latter is especially important because many development efforts must be made at the local government level. Also, the people must be so organised at the local level that they accept the national objectives determined at the centre and actively work toward their achievement. In other words, successful development in these fields depends on public cooperation, especially at the local level where development policies are mainly implemented. Such cooperation may take many forms, including provision for popular participation in the development process, especially in the making and execution of policies, and involvement of local governments in national development, as well as the establishment of national agencies responsible for assisting in the improvement of local government.

Besides improving the efficiency of administration, administrative decentralisation has the ability to bring development administrators and citizens closer to each other. A centralised administration tends to appear faceless as well as monolithic to the populace who therefore feel helpless toward it. On the other hand, evidence and experience has shown that administrative decentralisation results in less alienation and better understanding as well as more cooperation between development administrators and citizens (Khanna, 1975:382–83; Conyers, 1983:98–101).

Citizen participation in governmental decisions can become a very complicated issue and can take many forms. However, citizen participation is thought desirable in that it provides administrators with information on the policies and activities preferred by the people and thus makes the process of administering development much more efficient. Moreover, some authors have included "optimum participation among development's strategic principles because unless efforts are made to widen participation, development will interfere with men's quest for esteem and freedom from manipulation" (Goulet, 1977a:149). Other authors have argued that, "on balance, socio-economic development creates conditions favouring higher levels of participation" (Huntington and Nelson, 1976:52–53). It is apparent then that although there are different ways to view citizen participation, the dominant perspective in the literature is to treat it pragmatically, that is, to view it as a strategy to improve the development process (Bryant and White, 1982:211).

It can safely be assumed from currently available evidence that if participatory processes exist, the masses will want to get involved as long as they benefit from the process. Self-reliant development strategies facilitate participation and thus result in a better "fit" between what beneficiaries want and what the programmes provide. Participation thus facilitates implementation because the motivation to build and exploit the benefits are stronger when the participants have agreed upon the course of action (Paul, 1983:95–96).

That higher levels of participation of the citizenry should and do have positive effects on socioeconomic equality in the Third World is a foregone conclusion. More generally, widespread participation means more widespread access to power, and those who gain access to power will insist that there be actions to broaden their share in the economic benefits of society. In Jamaica, for example, participation of the citizenry in local organisations is closely tied to the benefits that members derive therefrom. And in China, where the socialist revolution was based on a large-scale participation of the peasants in a revolutionary struggle, economic cooperation in agriculture and sideline production were combined with the lowest level of government administration and the principles of collective ownership of land use and considerably strengthened the autonomous power of these local units of rural administration (Wertheim and Stiefel, 1982:83–85).

Hence, participation of the citizenry is not only a way to

improve programme performance but also a goal in itself. Some argue also that such participation should be encouraged because it is essential to self-reliance since all development activities must mobilise people's active participation so that they may be able to stand on their own feet (Gran, 1983:329–31).

Political Organisation and Leadership

The improvement of a nation's administrative capability is highly dependent on support from the political leadership. The role of the political leadership is indeed the most crucial factor to be ascertained in the process of national development (Tsurutani, 1973:25) and hence in the improvement in the administration of development. Political leadership is the arbiter of, rather than one participant or factor among many in, the process of national development. In most LDCs, the lack of the political leadership's role in support of major administrative change can be traced to have resulted from their own concern for maintaining their elite status and authority, which is so crisply controlled that it is difficult for society to penetrate.

Lending support to administrative change and reform requires, therefore, commitment on the part of the political leadership. Commitment here involves an overriding desire to promote rationality, rise of productivity, social and economic equalisation and improvement of institutions and attitudes. It is hoped that all of these aspects of national development combined will produce the administrative machinery needed and at the same time generate further change. The promotion of these ideals points toward modernisation and is directly opposed to the desire for the maintenance of the status quo. Not only should the political leadership be committed to these idieals in the interest of a just society and better development administration, but it should also be resolute enough to recognise such actions as helpful in resolving any problems pertaining to any identity crises.

If a country's leadership takes little interest in administration, downgrades administration in national priorities and is ambivalent about reform, reform agencies find themselves conducting technical exercises with little impact on administrative performance. This is less true of *ad hoc* task forces which depend less on elite support than professional acceptance (Caiden, 1973:340).

Economic and social development is dependent on effective statesmanship within a favourable political environment. Stagnant societies tend to reflect the lack of dynamic political organisation. Since development consists of social action and change, it requires both enlightened political leadership and the support of influential elements in the population. The two are significantly interrelated. Development cannot be successful without a sustaining philosophy of doctrine, political action of a dramatic order and effective organisation for the mobilisation of popular support.

Political leadership refers to that body of topmost decision makers whose legal or actual responsibility it is to make final authoritative decisions on each of the issues and problems it is concerned with. In this sense, political leadership, as a concept and category of analysis, is constant, while its actual membership or personnel composition is variable. Therefore, the structure of a government should be of a character that encourages responsible political action and facilitates the involvement of a wide cross section of the citizens in the development process. The character of the constitutional system and the relationships between political officials, on the one hand, and administrators, on the other, is thus an important element.

The political universe is the context of actions of political leadership; the political system is the major, yet manipulable, instrument that broadly structures and defines the behaviour of political leadership; and politics is the method by which the political leadership performs its role. It is thus that political leadership determines goals, selects methods and gives direction. Society develops or fails to develop according to the extent to which its political leadership is intelligent, creative, skillful and committed. Without this requisite function of political leadership, there will be no increase in administrative capability, no progress, no direction, no development.

The qualities necessary to exert administrative leadership

are as numerous as they are difficult to define. It is all very well to mention such traits as initiative, resourcefulness, ability, understanding and commitment as being necessary constituents of leadership, but it is impossible to construct a workable model made up of all the virtues deemed basic to the ideal political leader since certain patterns of leadership apply to certain, but not all, situations. A political leader may be successful in one situation, a failure in another. It can be said, however, that a political leader is successful if he or she can guide others toward a goal. This may involve administrative reform, getting essential work done on time, carrying out legislative mandates and so on. But in addition it can also mean the look into the future, the understanding of ultimate possibilities, the improvement of practices and the enlargement of the boundaries of action. The true political leader has some vision into the future as well as an eye for present reality.

Economic Development

Apart from the obvious need and advantages of economic growth, it influences the level of the administrative machinery. Government machinery and its operations are of the greatest consequences in developing countries, and the success or failure of the machinery hinges on the effectiveness of the development effort. Increasing levels of economic development would indicate the need for increasing levels of development administration which in turn influence the impact of development planning—since the secret of successful development planning lies not only in sensible politics but in good development administration (Lewis, 1966:preface). Moreover, higher levels of economic development do result in more revenue being available for the implementation of development projects and it also tends to increase the absorptive capacity of the country. With more readily available financial resources, government budgets can be properly augmented and the necessary inputs required for administering the development effort can be acquired.

Budgets play crucial roles in the development administration process because they entail a compulsory and direct transfer of resources. Hence, it is very important that the budget reflect the relative levels of resource allocation and capital formation to be achieved in the economy with respect to the existing revenue available.

The success of economic development planning depends to a significant degree upon the effectiveness of administration. K. William Kapp (1960) was not exaggerating when he indicated that a quantitatively inadequate or qualitatively defective system of development administration will not merely retard the development process but may defeat the entire development effort in an even more decisive manner than any temporary shortage of capital or an unfavourable monsoon. Thus, the strategic significance of development administration in economic development is to be found in the fact that it implements the plan, that it releases popular energy and initiative as well as community effort and that it channels latent propensities for cooperation and self-improvement into productive activities. To call development administration a strategic factor in economic development is not equivalent to considering it as the only factor or, for that matter, the primary cause. The process of growth and development is neither set nor kept in motion by one factor alone. Development administration is at best only one of several factors in economic growth. It is strategic in the sense that it influences and determines the success of the entire development plan and that it is susceptible to deliberate social control and change (Hope and Armstrong, 1980:320).

The role and significance of administration are greatly enhanced if economic growth becomes the objective of a deliberate economic plan. A national development plan is essentially a blueprint of public policies designed to bring about certain results which would not be forthcoming without it. Indeed, such a development plan may be said to be a decision determining the strategy of government action embodied in rules, regulations, controls, directives and impulses, all of which are designed to increase output and productivity. To be practical and effective, the plan must not only be a general scheme, but must have this scheme adequately worked out in detailed directives by careful planning of the different sectors, and it must give instructions for the specific inducements and controls by which the realisation of those directives becomes effected. It is clear why under these circumstances development administration assumes a key role in the development effort. Directives and controls must be applied, inducements have to be implemented and the progress and development process must be recorded and supervised so that the necessary adjustments can be enacted and effected as they become necessary. If governments assume these responsibilities of initiating, directing and promoting economic development through various policies and reforms designed to channel investments and to overcome structural obstacles and social rigidities, the establishment of an effective system of administration and an efficient civil service are bound to assume an unparalleled importance.

Coordination of administrative decisions concerning the allocation and investment of national resources must be an essential element of the development effort if it is to achieve its goals and objectives. The objective of the development effort should, therefore, be redefined to include the creation and expansion of administrative capability for resource mobilisation and plan implementation. Expansion of local government administrative capacity to identify and execute investments promoting growth with equity must also be given higher priority in national development policy.

DEVELOPMENT ADMINISTRATION IN THE CARIBBEAN: A CASE STUDY

Like most developing regions, development administration in the Caribbean was shaped primarily by the colonial overlords during their period of rule. The Caribbean nations are now independent, emergent Third World nations attempting to administer development projects for the provision of basic needs and the achievement of self-reliant growth. However, the process has been hampered by a number of factors, primary among which is the shortage of skilled bureaucrats and technocrats brought about by the "brain drain" phenomenon.

The highly trained individuals who emigrate consist of those persons, including students, who are likely to contribute actual or potential leadership in the intellectual, cultural, political and developmental spheres. Because of the phenomenon of externality, the country of emigration is always likely to suffer more than the immigrant country is likely to gain. Externality in this sense refers to the pervasive nature of education in the sense that the emigrant may increase productivity and welfare of others in the society, over and above what he or she is being paid for doing a job. This is the human capital contributive gain to the developed nations or the reverse transfer of technology, which has become a cause of preoccupation in the region to stop, and which is also one of the aims of the new international economic order (ILO, 1979:81).

In the Caribbean, the emigration of high-level manpower is a matter of great concern on account of the social, economic and cultural problems involved. Human abilities like leadership, initiative, and entrepreneurship are rare there and urgently needed; thus, emigration of those who possess them must be a blow to the development process there.

Emigration of high-level manpower from the Caribbean has traditionally been to the United Kingdom. However, in the aftermath of the 1962 ban on West Indian migration to the United Kingdom and the liberalisation of United States' immigration policy in 1965, the volume of Caribbean migration to the United States increased sharply. Migration to the United States as a percentage of the natural increase of the population during the period 1962–1976 averaged from a low of 7.4 percent from Guyana to a high of 37.8 percent from Barbados. The majority of these individuals were from the category of professional, technical and management (PTM) personnel. Annual migration from the PTM group represented roughly 10 percent of the incremental growth of manpower for that group in Jamaica, for example (Palmer, 1979:96). In Guyana, the same pattern prevailed but with a variance in the ethnic composition. Whereas in Jamaica the high-level manpower that emigrated was always predominantly Afro-Jamaican; in Guyana the emigrants are no longer Afro-Guyanese but Indo-Guyanese instead. This change in the ethnic composition of Guyanese emigrants occurred in the 1970s partly because of

THE DYNAMICS OF DEVELOPMENT

the sheer numbers of Indo-Guyanese in the labour force and partly for political reasons.

The emigration of high-level manpower has both a social and economic impact on the developing countries. In Trinidad and Tobago, for example, the losses and potential losses are quite substantial in relationship to the country's capacity to produce highly skilled individuals. The primary difficulty generated there comes from the loss of the critically few highly qualified and professional individuals, including students. These people contribute to national development not only by practicing their professions but also by serving in the capacity of teachers and intellectual leaders to promote development and change (Hope, 1976:211).

The importance of an integrated plan of manpower development on a long-term basis must therefore be stressed. The Caribbean countries need to review their manpower planning policies with special reference to the need for stimulating the return flow of personnel and effectively utilising the trained personnel currently available. Allowance should also be made for the individual need to find satisfactory and suitable reward.

Problems have also arisen because political interest in personnel matters has deteriorated into nepotism, pork-barrel appointments and the denial of jobs to nonsupporters of the governing party (Mills, 1970:15). This situation is particularly prevalent in Guyana where, for example, the late brilliant historian Dr. Walter Rodney was denied a teaching position at the University of Guyana primarily because of his opposition to the government of President Burnham. The relationship between politicians and development administrators in the Caribbean is aggravated by the highly personalised environment and the very sensitive political atmosphere in which political sympathies tend to be generally known and development administrators become overexposed in the political arena.

Personalised and centralised administrative structures and processes also imply that they are remote from popular penetration and influence and that they will inevitably serve as patronage institutions, not agents of change. Moreover, the type of centralisation that is characteristic of these Caribbean systems is not the coordinated type. It is the individual ministries and departments that are centralised and this gives rise to undercoordination and underpropulsion at the national policy level (Jones and Mills, 1976:330).

This pattern of structuring administrative institutions fully reflects an elite bias and indicates that greater coordination at the systemic level would be resisted by the vested interests. Institution building on completely different premises would certainly reduce the number of access points open to the vested interests and, possibly, would also reduce their capacity to make personal extractions from the system through fair or corrupt means (Jones, 1974a:268–86). This style of administrative institution building, therefore, makes it very difficult to modify effectiviely the status quo or to innovate (Jones and Mills, 1976:330).

The emergence of ministerial administration and the development of the cabinet system in the Caribbean have therefore significantly altered the role and, hence, the status of civil servants. From being the primary decision makers they have become the advisers; and evidently they have increasingly become advisers who are heard but seldom heeded. Thus, persons and groups seeking to influence policy increasingly direct their efforts toward the political actors. The politician is seen as the power figure and the civil servant falls into the perspective of a clerk (Nunes, 1974:353). But these politicians have no notion of "development" or "modernisation" or nation building and their major orientation is toward the preservation of law and order (Garcia-Zamor, 1977:38).

Leadership in the Caribbean, then, tends to be lacking. It has acted to maintain the inherited condition of the development of underdevelopment (Watson, 1975:44). Moreover, the decision-making power of the leadership in the Caribbean has been institutionalised informally over time and political expediency, induced by competitive politics, reinforces their dominance. They have, therefore, used this decision-making power in a conservative direction to maintain the status quo (Jones, 1974b:308).

Administrative reform in the Caribbean is overdue. Such

reform must result in a development administration machinery that can elicit cooperative action to implement government policy in an uncertain environment for maximum social gain (Hope, 1983b). Moreover, the reform program must result in the creation and acquisition of a cadre of skilled and effective administrators who are not politically obstructed in their attempts to implement development policy. Additionally, the administrative reform must result in administrative structures that are compatible in their functions, as well as their very structures, and with the demands of the New International Economic Order. It is also vital that the administrative apparatus should not constitute a screen separating the political authorities from the citizens. The state must, therefore, be more firmly rooted in the people. This is in accordance with the formal requirements of the NIEO. If the Caribbean nations are to be able to implement the NIEO, they must begin by changing themselves in accordance with the principles of the new order that they seek to establish. As such, the advocacy here is for reform leading to the practice of strategic management. Recent evidence indicates that development programs succeed when the leaders and managers are able to practice strategic management (Paul, 1982:232). Accomplishing such management requires both structural and process interventions. Structural interventions are the most frequently advocated and much has been written on the subject. Included are integrative mechanisms, organisational autonomy and decentralisation. Much less has been written on the process interventions, which include human resource development and planning and participation of the citizenry.

Process interventions need to be taken seriously by Caribbean governments. In some of the nations (for example, Grenada), there have been attempts to build a system of "participatory democracy" involving wider mobilisation of the people within community councils and village assemblies (Hope, 1983b:55). However, these initiatives have met with marginal success primarily because they were advocated more as a strategy of political mobilisation rather than a strategy of development administration. In the Eastern Caribbean region, citizen participation mirrors a continuum of varied behaviour ranging from manipulation to tokenism. There is no substantive participation. Participation is undermined and diluted by the colonial ethos and persistent traditionality of top-heavy, closed-model management which perpetuates bureaucratic centralisation (Khan, 1982:102–5). The type of administrative reform required in the Caribbean must, therefore, be both macro and micro in nature. Macro reforms are those that include the entire administrative system. Micro reforms are those that take place within a given institution. Historically, and for reasons of scale, micro reforms have been frequently attempted in the LDCs. However, this should not be regarded as sufficient reason to pursue only micro reforms. Macro reforms must also be tackled as part of any overall national movement to restructure the administrative machinery. Moreover, micro reforms by themselves tend to come off as piecemeal and fragmented and may do more harm than good to the existing administrative structure.

4

Summary and Conclusions

The concepts of development and development administration are inextricably intertwined. A nation is bound to remain underdeveloped unless the necessary administrative machinery is in place to implement the development strategy. But, development is a relative concept. From the standpoint of the Third World developing nations it is not just a matter of economics. It encompasses the social, political, cultural and environmental elements as well. As such, those economists who base their policy advice simply on growth models, which emphasise capital formation, take too many things for granted. The developing nations, on the other hand, see development as a bottom-up process that entails the transfer of appropriate technology for the provision of basic needs, at least. Moreover, they would like to see this accomplished within the framework of a New International Economic Order.

This new development strategy, which also reflects a fair degree of consensus among scholars, places a great amount of emphasis on collective self-reliance. However, it is recognised that the cooperation of the industrialised countries looms large. But the response of the rich nations to the challenge is not to be found in development aid alone. It is the total relationship, the nature of the overall policies of the rich nations that is relevant (Streeten, 1979b:52).

The administration of development in the LDCs is still a legacy of their colonial past. The colonial political system was a mere bureaucratic system. It was centralised and no separate institution for political and administrative functions existed. This created a blurred distinction between the "administrative" and the "political" and the result was obviously a highly stagnant bureaucracy. Policy was largely formulated and implemented by the colonial overlords and their chosen subordinates. The bureaucratic colonial administration has now been replaced by native politicians who also exercise centralised authority and control. Politics is now the order of the day and the development administration machinery is in a state of ineptness.

It is therefore quite evident that the creation of a suitable machinery for the administration of development in the LDCs is of vital necessity and should be made a priority endeavour. The success of such an endeavour depends on a number of factors, as outlined in this work. The expanded role of government into social and economic areas has increasingly demanded new and improved conceptual and operational frameworks so that national development is manageable and practicable. However, while the need for rapid development has been vividly felt and national programmes for the satisfaction of these growth needs have been constructed and articulated, less attention has been devoted to the requirements of programme implementation, including the operational characteristics and the organisation systems through which these end goals are attainable.

Effective administration needs autonomous, yet interdependent, centres of activity that can provide resources for and exact performances from each other. A healthy economic system, a strong political organisation and leadership, proper manpower planning and training and effective decentralisation and communication are all necessary for improving administration. Otherwise, bureaucracy takes over at the expense of society and a "big push" in the entire society would then be needed to develop independence from the bureaucracy.

Development administration has a great part to play in the development effort. It can supply the facts, apply the methods and evaluate the record. It need not assume responsibility for making overall plans for a better society, but it can and should be in a position to stimulate, support and carry out plans that are politically accepted. It is the instrument of accomplishment and is characterised by its purposes, its loyalties and its attitudes. Its purposes are to stimulate and facilitate defined programs of social and economic progress. They are purposes of change, innovation and movement as contrasted with purposes of maintaining the status quo as currently exists in the LDCs (Gant, 1979:20). Without a proper machinery of development administration, all strategies of development applied in the developing nations are doomed to failure and their external economic dependence would persist.

Development then is not the result simply of applying theories, models or strategies but is an integral part of the dynamic process of society's growth as a whole. Moreover, the aspect of administering that development has a direct impact on the nature and structure of the change effected through the development process.

Development administration is targeted on the design and implementation of structures and procedures to facilitate development. Analysing the problems and the solutions to development administration improvement therefore presupposes the need for change. As such, development administration studies are aimed at a relatively high-level target audience. These are the people who can affect the procedures and structures through which development plans will be implemented. They make the policies that others must live with (Honadle and Klauss, 1979:210).

Thus, development administration involves the establishment of new agencies and the reorientation of existing agencies to discharge the enormous responsibilities and to perform the several and complex functions of economic development—an increasingly complex set of functions given the current approaches to development. These new approaches to development resulted from the developing nations' dissatisfaction with the present world economic order. They are demanding change and they seek to do so through either unilateral action or by a process of negotiation with the developed world. The developing nations consider the prevailing rules and practices governing the working of the international economy to be inequitable and discriminatory, in a cumulative way, in favour of the developed nations which have a greater command over resources and technology. Moreover, the disparity in income and wealth between the developed and developing nations, instead of narrowing as a result of the working of the international economic system, continues to be large and widening.

As a result of these experiences, the leaders in the developing nations have realised that the benefits of growth are marginal and do not trickle down and, therefore, what is needed is a direct attack on mass poverty based on the satisfaction of basic human needs (Haq, 1976:27–28) and assisted through the transfer of appropriate technology.

The countries of the developing world share common experiences and aspirations in their relationships with the developed world. These have contributed to the sense of cohesion and the growth of united efforts on the part of the developing nations in their struggle for a New International Economic Order, which is concerned not only with obtaining a greater share of the world's resources for themselves but also with obtaining a greater role in the decision-making processes in the international institutions, such as the World Bank and the International Monetary Fund which set the rules of international economic relations (Islam, 1979:179).

Through a New International Economic Order, resources are expected to be redistributed and both technological and economic dependence are expected to be reduced since there will be a reduction in the use of scarce resources to import basic production goods (Dowidar, 1975:52). In general, the developing nations want to bring the rules and practices governing the international flow of commodities, labour, capital and technology under broad international control and away from unilateral determination by the developed nations as has been the case hitherto. It is hoped that such an accomplishment would move the developing nations closer to their goal of achieving a development that provides basic needs and that is conceived from a value perspective totally different from the type of organisation that perpetuated underdevelopment.

It seems rather obvious, therefore, that what the LDCs are struggling for at this point in time is equality of opportunity and not equality of income. The developing nations are not seeking the income levels of the rich nations. They are only suggesting that their societies be given a fair chance to develop on an equal basis without systematic exploitation or discrimination. They are simply requesting the reconstruction of the international economic order to a more egalitarian, democratic and self-reliantly propelled one so that development proceeds without dependence and provides basic needs. It must be pointed out, however, that the conceptual work makes it clear that the pursuit of basic needs is not a distinct development strategy in itself. It can only be regarded as a principal objective of development that can be achieved through a New International Economic Order. The distinct emphasis that the basic-needs objective provides is a heightened concern for the achievement of the ultimate goals of the whole population. Put another way, explicitly adopting the meeting of basic needs as an important objective of development draws attention to the ultimate goals of the society and the ways in which policies are geared to meeting these goals.

The debates on the NIEO and the basic-needs approach to development have not been without controversy. There is a contradiction between the centre (the countries of the North) and the periphery (the nations of the South). This contradiction was brought about by historical circumstances but is still being built into the world structure. The developing nations are calling for a NIEO while the developed nations are not all keen on a NIEO but rather regard the present world system as adequate. The developed nations, at the same time, support the basic needs approach outside of a NIEO framework. Despite this apparent contradiction, though, there is indeed compatibility between the NIEO and the basic-needs approach. This compatibility stems from the emphasis on self-reliance. Self-reliance is regarded here as autonomy of decision making and full mobilisation of a society's own resources under its own initiative and direction. To the extent, therefore, that the developed nations are willing to accept this, there ought to be no fundamental conflict between the provision of basic needs and increased resource flows brought about by an NIEO. The real task is the negotiation of a world economic system that benefits both the people of the South and the people of the North. A system that results in peace, social justice and economic well-being.

North-South relations should be exhaustively reassessed with a view to achieving a mutually acceptable regulated and planned interdependence. A harmonisation of currently conflicting objectives and lasting solutions must be worked out not only within the existing political, social, economic and value systems and must take into account the possible changes that may be foreseen, particularly within the context of collective self-reliance (Hope, 1982d:13–14).

Collective self-reliance, by enhancing the position of the developing nations, can give real meaning to the concept of interdependence. So far it has meant dominance on one side and dependence on the other. Only structural changes resulting in the reduction of inequalities among nations and the redistribution of resources can make global interdependence useful and desirable to all partners in development for lasting development. The cornerstone of a strategy of self-reliant development is that economic activity should be geared to the satisfaction of basic needs of the masses. Moreover, the developing nations and their masses are the best arbiters of their own basic needs and the order of priority in which these needs should be satisfied. Collectively, the interests of the various developing nations are balanced against each other so as to make it profitable for each country to accept the deal as a whole.

A self-reliant approach to economic development with central emphasis on meeting the basic needs of the majority of the population of the developing nations provides a fresh orientation in development strategy. It implies an unprecedented expansion in the production of foodstuffs and of simple manufactured goods, using technology appropriate to the resource endowments of the developing nations themselves. Since the pattern of basic needs in developing nations is quite different from the pattern of import demand by developed nations, the adoption of a basic-needs strategy of development would mean the emergence of a new pattern of industrialisation in the developing nations.

The concept of accelerated economic development through

self-reliance or collective self-reliance is not a new one. Until recently, however, that concept found expression in integration schemes of a regional or subregional character, which currently embrace about one-half of the total number of developing nations. Within the framework of these integration schemes, considerable progress has been made in expanding the mutual trade of the member countries, in developing complementary industries and in general harmonisation of their development programmes. In some subregional groupings, also, important initiatives have been taken to improve the bargaining power of the member countries in their dealings with transnational corporations and to regulate the operations of these corporations.

The new awareness on the part of the developing nations of the need to strengthen their mutual economic relations provides a unique opportunity for building a global system of economic cooperation among Third World nations based on the valuable experience gained so far on a regional and subregional basis. Thus, closer economic cooperation among developing nations would improve their bargaining power in their economic relations with developed nations as well as transnational corporations. It would also provide, to a much greater extent than hitherto, the means for accelerating their economic and social development through their own efforts. It must be pointed out, however, that changes in the present international economic order are essentially a function of power relationships. The current state of the dialogue indicates that there may be little hope for modification of that order unless the countries of the South further consolidate their own economic power base. They attempted to do so with the oil embargo of 1973. But certainly such measures are a bit drastic. The developed nations of the North, however, should give recognition to such a fact and attempt to negotiate in good faith a New International Economic Order.

In all fairness it must be stated that the governments of the developed nations have differed in their responses to the claims for a New International Economic Order. The United States has tended to be the most resistant to the various proposals to change while Europe and Japan were more accommodating in their responses, perhaps because of their greater dependence on imported materials from the primary producing nations of the South. The general state of affairs is one where the Northern nations are somewhat skeptical of the proposals for a NIEO but differ among themselves in their willingness to discuss the various proposals. Recently though, there have been signs of an increased willingness to continue to dialogue with the United States participating as a full member of the Northern group of nations. Such was evident with President Reagan's attendance at the North-South Cancun Summit in Mexico on international cooperation and development, October 22–23, 1981.

Of major importance in the achievement of development is the method and the mix of policies adapted to finance it. In the LDCs there has been a major shift toward the acquisition of development finance from private sources. Among private creditors there has been a shift toward lending through financial markets and away from lending by suppliers. Indeed, debt to suppliers increased more slowly than debt to official agencies. Suppliers' credits had emerged as an important source of finance in the 1960s as suppliers and their governments took measures to assist their own export businesses. Although borrowers were increasingly able to handle debt on commercial terms, some excesses in this area did lead to debt difficulties. Banks became more active as lenders to developing nations in the early 1970s. Borrowers increasingly substituted loans from them for suppliers' credits. These loans were not only competitive in price, but offered advantages of ease of arrangement, flexibility of use and quick disbursement and were not necessarily tied to specific purchases.

The increased availability of loans from private banks was facilitated by institutional developments in the international financial markets in the early 1970s. These developments permitted a growing pool of short-term funds to be transformed into long-term loans without the previous risks. The syndicated floating rate bank credit transferred the risk of interest rate fluctuations from lenders to borrowers. Through the practice of syndication, a wholesale market could be developed, lowering costs, while large sums could be raised at the same time that exposure of any one lender arising from a single transaction could be reduced. The growth of an international interbank deposit and money market facilitated the funding of loans, particularly for banks lending in other than their home currencies (Katz, 1979:10–11).

The 1970s have also seen a rapid growth of the international or Eurobond market, which together with the growth of foreign issues in national bond markets, has provided an increasing source of funds for a limited number of developing nations. Total issues in these markets, including both public issues and privately placed bonds, increased sixfold during the 1970s and now account for nearly 40 percent of the outstanding debt of developing nations (Brandt, 1980:222). Most of these private loans have gone to a few middle-income countries with a concomitant increase in their debt-servicing burden. As a result, these debtor economies and the entire international credit structure are now very vulnerable to any disruptions in the flows of capital, which can be caused by a greater demand for credit in the North, by a borrowing country being regarded as less creditworthy, by insufficient bank capital or by the actions of regulatory authorities (Brandt, 1980:223).

The issue with the debt problem is that a very large proportion of funds are lent on terms that are onerous for borrowers from the point of view of both the repayment capacity and the time the developing nations need to correct structural problems in their balance of payments. This is particularly true for the low-income nations. In these nations, the level and pattern of future debt service precludes taking on significant new amounts of debt on other than concessional terms in the context of their overall development programs while the middle-income countries need loans on longer maturities.

The developing nations also need better access to capital markets. This would ensure that funds transferred are on better terms than they otherwise would have been, that the distribution of capital flows among developing nations is improved, that the funds can be disbursed rapidly and that the existing structure of international capital flows is not weakened. Furthermore, improved access to capital markets would also serve to improve the maturity, structure, and stability of capital flows to developing nations and help forestall liquidity crises. Improvements are also desirable in the mechanisms and procedures to deal with such situations when they occur.

Finally, this work has shown that to achieve development, irrespective of the strategy followed, the development administration machinery must be compatible in terms of its ability and capability to perform the task within the overall developmental thrust. It was also shown that the theory and practice of development is very complex and has evolved through several phases encompassing the purely economic model at one extreme to the more humanistic model at the present time. Furthermore, there are similarities in the traditions of development practice and theory and the evolution of traditions in development administration. Both development administration and development theory tend to be centralising, authoritative and technological in character. Both have come to a recognition of the need for developing legitimacy and of the importance of the role of citizen involvement in their processes and practice. The current strategies of development, however, place greater emphasis on participation of the masses for the achievement of basic needs. That is, they are strategies of egalitarian development (Griffin and James, 1981:7) with primary emphasis on redistribution of income in favour of the poor.

References

Abdel-Fadil, M.; Francis Cripps; and John Wells. (1977). "A New International Economic Order," *Cambridge Journal of Economics*, vol. 1, no. 2 (June):205–13.

Ahmad, Muzaffer. (1982). "Political Economy of Public Enterprise." In *Public Enterprise in Less-Developed Countries*. Ed. Leroy P. Jones. New York: Cambridge University Press.

Alderfer, Harold F. (1967). *Public Administration in Newer Nations*. New York: Praeger.

Anstee, Margaret J. (1981). "Some Major Issues in Public Administration for Development." In *International Perspectives in Public Administration*. Ed. E. N. Scott. Canberra, Australia: College of Advanced Education.

Armstrong, Aubrey B. (1980). "Management Development and Training in Public Enterprises in Developing Countries: A Look at Policy and Strategy." In *Managing Training and Training Managers in Public Enterprises in Developing Countries*. Ed. Aubrey Armstrong and Stane Mozina. Ljubljana, Yugoslavia: International Centre for Public Enterprises in Developing Countries.

Arndt, H. W. (1981). "Economic Development: A Semantic History," *Economic Development and Cultural Change*, vol. 29, no. 3 (April):457–66.

Bahl, Roy. (1972). "A Representative Tax System Approach to Measuring Tax Effort in Developing Countries," *IMF Staff Papers*, vol. 19, no. 1 (March):97–122.

Balog, Nikola. (1966). *Administrative Management of Public Enterprises*. Brussels: International Institute of Administrative Sciences.

Baster, Nancy, ed. (1972). *Measuring Development: The Role and Adequacy of Development Indicators*. London: Frank Cass and Company.

Bird, Richard. (1976). "Assessing Tax Performance in Developing Countries: A Critical Review of the Literature," *Finanzarchiv*, n.f. 34, heft 2:244–65.

―――. (1983). "Income Tax Reform in Developing Countries: The Administrative Dimension," *Bulletin for International Fiscal Documentation*, vol. 37, no. 1 (January):3–14.

Bird, Richard, and Luc De Wulf. (1973). "Taxation and Income Distribution in Latin America: A Critical Review of Empirical Studies," *IMF Staff Papers*, vol. 20, no. 3 (November):639–82.

Brandt, Willy. (1980). *North-South: A Program for Survival: The Report of the Independent Commission on International Development Issues*. Cambridge, Mass.: M.I.T. Press.

Bryant, Coralie, and Louise G. White. (1980). *Managing Rural Development*. West Hartford, Conn.: Kumarian Press.

―――. (1982). *Managing Development in the Third World*. Boulder, Colo.: Westview Press.

Caiden, Gerald E. (1973). "Development, Administrative Capacity and Administrative Reform," *International Review of Administrative Sciences*, vol. 39, no. 4:327–44.

Castro, Fidel. (1983). *The World Economic and Social Crisis*. Havana: Council of State Publishing House.

Chelliah, Raja J. (1971). "Trends in Taxation in Developing Countries," *IMF Staff Papers*, vol. 18, no. 2 (July):254–327.

Chelliah, Raja J.; H. J. Baas; and M. R. Kelly. (1975). "Tax Ratios and Tax Effort in Developing Countries, 1969–71," *IMF Staff Papers*, vol. 22, no. 1 (March):187–205.

Chenery, H. B., and A. M. Strout. (1966). "Foreign Assistance and Economic Development," *American Economic Review*, vol. 56, no. 4 (September):670–733.

Chikulo, B. C. (1981). "The Zambian Administrative Reforms: An Alternative View," *Public Administration and Development*, vol. 1, no. 1 (January-March):55–65.

Clower, Robert; George Dalton; Mitchell Harwitz; and A. A. Walters. (1966). *Growth without Development*. Evanston, Ill.: Northwestern University Press.

Cody, John; Helen Hughes; and David Wall, eds. (1980). *Policies for Industrial Progress in Developing Countries*. New York: Oxford University Press.

Conyers, Diana. (1983). "Decentralization: The Latest Fashion in Development Administration," *Public Administration and Development*, vol. 3, no. 2 (April-June):97–109.

Corea, Gamani. (1981). *Need for Change: Towards the New International Economic Order*. New York: Pergamon Press.

Dabasi-Schweng, L. (1965). "The Influence of Economic Factors." In *Public Administration in Developing Countries*. Ed. Martin Kriesberg. Washington, D.C.: Brookings Institution.

Dhonte, Pierre. (1979). *Clockwork Debt*. Lexington, Mass.: D. C. Heath.

Dowidar, Mohamed. (1975). "Economic Development in the Dependent World." In *World Inequality*. Ed. Immanuel Wallerstein. Montreal: Black Rose Books.

Dube, S. C. (1964). "Bureaucracy and Nation-Building in Transitional Societies," *International Social Science Journal*, vol. 16, no. 2:229–36.

Dunkerley, Harold B. (1977). "The Choice of Appropriate Technologies," *Finance and Development*, vol. 14, no. 3 (September):36–39.

Dwivedi, O. P. and J. Nef. (1982). "Crises and Continuities in Development Theory and Administration: First and Third World Perspectives," *Public Administration and Development*, vol. 2, no. 1 (January-March):59–77.

Eckaus, Richard. (1977). *Appropriate Technologies for Developing Countries*. Washington, D.C.: National Academy of Sciences.

Erb, Guy F. (1975). "The Developing World's Challenge in Perspective." In *Beyond Dependency: The Developing World Speaks Out*. Ed. Guy F. Erb and Valeriana Kallab. Washington, D.C.: Overseas Development Council.

Ernst, Dieter. (1981). "Technology Policy for Self-Reliance: Some Major Issues," *International Social Science Journal*, vol. 33, no. 3:466–80.

Fainsod, Merle. (1963). "The Structure of Development Administration." In *Development Administration: Concepts and Problems*. Ed. Irving Swerdlow. Syracuse, N.Y.: Syracuse University Press.

Fields, Gary S. (1980). *Poverty, Inequality, and Development*. New York: Cambridge University Press.

Flammang, Robert A. (1979). "Economic Growth and Economic Development: Counterparts or Competitors," *Economic Development and Cultural Change*, vol. 28, no. 1 (October):47–61.

Fleming, Alexander. (1981). *Private Capital Flows to Developing Countries and Their Determination*. Washington, D.C.: World Bank Staff Working Paper no. 484.

Frank, André Gunder. (1975). *On Capitalist Underdevelopment*. Bombay: Oxford University Press.

———. (1981). *Crisis: In the Third World*. New York: Holmes and Meier.

114   REFERENCES

Galtung, Johan. (1978). *Self-Reliance and Global Interdependence.* Ottawa: Canadian International Development Agency.
———. (1979). *Development, Environment and Technology: Towards a Technology for Self-Reliance.* New York: United Nations.
———. (1980). *The North/South Debate: Technology, Basic Human Needs and the New International Economic Order.* New York: Institute for World Order, Working Paper no. 12.
Galtung, Johan; Peter O'Brien; and Roy Preiswerk, eds. (1980). *Self-Reliance: A Strategy for Development.* Geneva: Institute for Development Studies.
Gant, George F. (1966). "A Note on Application of Development Administration," *Public Policy,* vol. 15:199–211.
———. (1979). *Development Administration: Concepts, Goals, Methods.* Madison: University of Wisconsin Press.
Garcia-Zamor, Jean-Claude. (1973). "Micro-Bureaucracies and Development Administration," *International Review of Administrative Sciences,* vol. 39, no. 4:417–23.
———. (1977). *The Ecology of Development Administration in Jamaica, Trinidad and Tobago, and Barbados.* Washington, D.C.: Organisation of American States.
Ghai, D. P.; A. R. Khan; E.L.H. Lee; and T. Alfthan. (1977). *The Basic-Needs Approach to Development.* Geneva: International Labour Organisation.
Gillis, Malcolm. (1980). "The Role of State Enterprises in Economic Development," *Social Research,* vol. 47 (Summer):248–89.
Gillis, Malcolm; Dwight H. Perkins; Michael Roemer; and Donald R. Snodgrass. (1983). *Economics of Development.* New York: Norton.
Goulet, Denis. (1971). "Development or Liberation," *International Development Review,* vol. 13, no. 3:6–10.
———. (1977a). *The Cruel Choice: A New Concept in the Theory of Development.* New York: Atheneum.
———. (1977b). *The Uncertain Promise: Value Conflicts in Technology Transfer.* Washington, D.C.: Overseas Development Council.
Gran, Guy. (1983). *Development by People.* New York: Praeger.
Griffin, Keith, and John Enos. (1970a). "Foreign Assistance: Objectives and Consequences," *Economic Development and Cultural Change,* vol. 18, no. 3 (April):313–27.
———. (1970b). *Planning Development.* London: Addison-Wesley.
Griffin, Keith, and Jeffrey James. (1981). *The Transition to Egalitarian Development.* New York: St. Martin's Press.

Guha, Ashok S. (1981). *An Evolutionary View of Economic Growth.* New York: Oxford University Press.

Hammergren, Linn A. (1983). *Development and the Politics of Administrative Reform.* Boulder, Colo.: Westview Press.

Hanson, A. H. (1965). *Public Enterprise and Economic Development.* London: Routledge and Kegan Paul.

Haq, Mahbub ul. (1976). *The Poverty Curtain: Choices for the Third World.* New York: Columbia University Press.

———. (1980). "An International Perspective on Basic Needs," *Finance and Development,* vol. 17, no. 3 (September):11–14.

Heady, Ferrel. (1966). *Public Administration: A Comparative Perspective.* Englewood-Cliffs, N.J.: Prentice-Hall.

Healey, Derek T. (1972). "Development Policy: New Thinking about an Interpretation," *Journal of Economic Literature,* vol. 10, no. 3 (September):757–97.

Heaphey, James, ed. (1971). *Spatial Dimensions of Development Administration.* Durham, N.C.: Duke University Press.

Heeger, Gerald A. (1974). *The Politics of Underdevelopment.* New York: St. Martin's Press.

Helleiner, Gerald K. (1979). "International Technology Issues: Southern Needs and Northern Responses." In *Mobilising Technology for World Development.* Ed. Jairam Ramesh and Charles Weiss. New York: Praeger.

Heper, Metin. (1975). "Notes on Public Administration Training for the Potential Bureaucratic Elites of the Transitional Societies," *International Social Science Journal,* vol. 27, no. 1:163–73.

Honadle, George, and Rudi Klauss. (1979). "Summary and Conclusion: Recipes for More Practical Planning in the Face of Uncertainty." In *International Development Administration: Implementation Analysis for Development Projects.* Ed. George Honadle and Rudi Klauss. New York: Praeger.

Honey, John C. (1968). *Toward Strategies for Public Administration Development in Latin America.* Syracuse, N.Y.: Syracuse University Press.

Hope, Kempe Ronald. (1976). "The Emigration of High-Level Manpower from Developing to Developed Countries with Reference to Trinidad and Tobago," *International Migration,* vol. 14, no. 3:209–18.

———. (1977a). "Development Administration in Post-independence Guyana," *International Review of Administrative Sciences,* vol. 43, no. 1:67–72.

———. (1977b). "Taxation in Developing Countries," *Bulletin for*

International Fiscal Documentation, vol. 31, no. 11 (November):493–99.

―――. (1979a). "Development and Development Administration: Perspectives and Dimensions," *Administrative Change*, vol. 7, no. 1 (July-December):11–24.

―――. (1979b). *Development Policy in Guyana: Planning, Finance, and Administration*. Boulder, Colo.: Westview Press.

―――. (1980). "The Role of Domestic Savings in the Financing of Economic Development in Developing Countries," *Economic Affairs*, vol. 25, no. 11 (November):257–64.

―――. (1981a). "Agriculture and Economic Development in the Caribbean," *Food Policy*, vol. 6, no. 4 (November):253–65.

―――. (1981b). "The Concept of Economic Development: Toward a New Interpretation," *Man and Development*, vol. 3, no. 2 (June):77–82.

―――. (1982a). "Improving Public Enterprise Management in Developing Countries," *Journal of General Management*, vol. 7, no. 3 (Spring):72–85.

―――. (1982b). "The New International Economic Order, Basic Needs, and Technology Transfer: Toward an Integrated Strategy for Development in the Future," *World Futures*, vol. 18, nos. 3,4:163–76.

―――. (1982c). "The Role of Savings in the Financing of Economic Development in the Caribbean," *Savings and Development*, vol. 6, no. 4:381–91.

―――. (1982d). "Self-Reliant Development in the Third World," *Transnational Perspectives*, vol. 8, no. 4:13–15.

―――. (1983a). "The Administration of Development in Developing Nations Revisited," *Public Administration Review*, vol. 21, no. 1 (January-June).

―――. (1983b). "The Administration of Development in Emergent Nations: The Problems in the Caribbean," *Public Administration and Development*, vol. 3, no. 1 (January-March):49–59.

―――. (1983c). "Basic Needs and Technology Transfer Issues in the New International Economic Order," *American Journal of Economics and Sociology*, vol. 42, no. 4 (October): 393–403.

―――. (1983d). "Some Problems of Administering Development in Developing Nations," *Indian Journal of Public Administration*, vol. 29, no. 1 (January-March):1–10.

―――. (1983e). "Self–Reliance and Participation of the Poor in the Development Process in the Third World," *Futures*, vol. 15, no. 6 (December): 455–462.

Hope, Kempe Ronald, and Aubrey Armstrong. (1980). "Toward the Development of Administrative and Management Capability in Developing Countries," *International Review of Administrative Sciences*, vol. 46, no. 4:315–21.

Howard, John B. (1982). "Social Accountability of Public Enterprises: Law and Community Controls in the New Development Strategies." In *Public Enterprise in Less-Developed Countries*. Ed. Leroy P. Jones. New York: Cambridge University Press.

Hughes, Helen. (1980). "Achievements and Objectives of Industrialisation." In *Policies for Industrial Progress in Developing Countries*. Eds. John Cody; Helen Hughes; and David Wall. New York: Oxford University Press.

Hunter, Robert. (1971). *What Is Development?* Washington, D.C.: Overseas Development Council.

Huntington, Samuel P., and Joan M. Nelson. (1976). *No Easy Choice: Political Participation in Developing Countries*. Cambridge: Harvard University Press.

International Labour Office. (1976). *Employment, Growth and Basic Needs: A One-World Problem*. Geneva: ILO.

———. (1977). *Meeting Basic Needs: Strategies for Eradicating Mass Poverty and Unemployment: Conclusions of the World Employment Conference 1976*. Geneva: ILO.

———. (1978). *Technology, Employment and Basic Needs*. Geneva: ILO.

———. (1979). *Growth, Employment and Basic Needs in Latin America and the Caribbean*. Geneva: ILO.

International Monetary Fund. (1974). *IMF Survey, June 3*. Washington, D.C.: IMF.

Islam, Nurul. (1979). "Revolt of the Periphery." In *Toward a New Strategy for Development: A Rothko Chapel Colloqium*. Ed. K. Q. Hill. New York: Pergamon Press.

———. (1981). "Economic Interdependence between Rich and Poor Nations," *Third World Quarterly*, vol. 3, no. 2 (April):230–50.

Jetha, Nizar. (1981). "Some Problems of Tax Policy in Developing Countries," *Bulletin for International Fiscal Documentation*, vol. 35, no. 10 (October):448–55.

Jones, Edwin. (1974a). "Administrative Institution-Building in Jamaica: An Interpretation," *Social and Economic Studies*, vol. 23, no. 2 (June):264–91.

———. (1974b). "Some Notes on Decision-Making and Change in Caribbean Administrative Systems," *Social and Economic Studies*, vol. 23, no. 2 (June):292–310.

Jones, Edwin, and G. E. Mills. (1976). "Institutional Innovation and Change in the Commonwealth Caribbean," *Social and Economic Studies*, vol. 25, no. 4 (December):323–46.

Jones, Leroy, ed. (1982). *Public Enterprise in Less-Developed Countries*. New York: Cambridge University Press.

Kapp, K. William. (1960). "Economic Development, National Planning and Public Administration," *Kyklos*, vol. 13, fasc. 2:172–201.

Kasdan, Alan R. (1973). *The Third World: A New Focus for Development*. Cambridge, Mass.: Schenkman.

Katz, Jeffrey. (1979). *Capital Flows and Developing Country Debt*. Washington, D.C.: World Bank Staff Working Paper no. 352.

Khan, Jamal. (1982). *Public Management: The Eastern Caribbean Experience*. Leiden, Netherlands: Royal Institute of Linguistics and Anthropology.

Khanna, B. S. (1975). "Citizen and Administration," *Indian Journal of Public Administration*, vol. 21, no. 3 (April-June):377–90.

Korten, David C., and Felipe B. Alfonso, eds. (1983). *Bureaucracy and the Poor: Closing the Gap*. West Hartford, Conn.: Kumarian Press.

Kuzmin, S. A. (1977). "An Integrated Approach to Development and Employment," *International Labour Review*, vol. 115, no. 3 (May-June):327–41.

Lappé, Frances Moore; Joseph Collins; and David Kinley. (1981). *Aid as Obstacle*. San Francisco: Institute for Food and Development Policy.

Laszlo, Ervin; Robert Baker, Jr.; Elliott Eisenberg; and Venkata Raman. (1978). *The Objectives of the New International Economic Order*. New York: Pergamon Press.

Leff, Nathaniel. (1979). "International Transfer of Technology to Developing Countries: Implications for U.S. Policy." In *Technology and Economic Development: A Realistic Perspective*. Ed. Samuel M. Rosenblatt. Boulder, Colo.: Westview Press.

Leipziger, Danny M. (1981). "The Basic Human Needs Approach and North-South Relations." In *The Challenge of the New International Economic Order*. Ed. Edwin P. Reubens. Boulder, Colo.: Westview Press.

Lewis, W. Arthur. (1966). *Development Planning*. London: Allen and Unwin.

Lindenberg, Marc, and Benjamin Crosby. (1981). *Managing Development: The Political Dimension*. West Hartford, Conn.: Kumarian Press.

Lisk, Franklyn. (1977). "Conventional Development Strategies and

Basic Needs Fulfillment," *International Labour Review*, vol. 115, no. 2 (March-April):175–91.

Little, Ian M. D. (1982). *Economic Development: Theory, Policy, and International Relations*. New York: Basic Books.

Loup, Jacques. (1983). *Can the Third World Survive?* Baltimore, Md.: Johns Hopkins University Press.

McGinnis, James B. (1979). *Bread and Justice: Toward a New International Economic Order*. New Jersey: Paulist Press.

McRobie, George. (1979). "Intermediate Technology: Small Is Beautiful," *Third World Quarterly*, vol. 1, no. 2 (April):71–86.

Martin, Alison, and W. A. Lewis. (1956). "Patterns of Public Revenue and Expenditure," *Manchester School*, vol. 24, no. 3 (September):203–44.

Mikesell, Raymond F. (1983). *The Economics of Foreign Aid and Self-sustaining Development*. Boulder, Colo.: Westview Press.

Mills, G. E. (1966). "Education and Training for the Public Service in the West Indies," *Journal of Administration Overseas*, vol. 5, no. 3 (July):155–66.

———. (1970). "Public Administration in the Commonwealth Caribbean: Evolution, Conflicts and Challenges," *Social and Economic Studies*, vol. 19, no. 1 (March):5–25.

———. (1973). "The Environment of Commonwealth Caribbean Bureaucracies," *International Review of Administrative Sciences*, vol. 39, no. 1:14–24.

Muhammad, Faqir. (1974). "A Change of Orientation in Public Administration Training." In *Public Administration Training for the Less Developed Countries*. Ed. Irving Swerdlow and Marcus Ingle. Syracuse, N.Y.: Maxwell School of Citizenship and Public Affairs, Syracuse University.

Munoz, Heraldo, ed. (1981). *From Dependency to Development: Strategies to Overcome Underdevelopment and Inequality*. Boulder, Colo.: Westview Press.

Murdoch, William W. (1980). *The Poverty of Nations*. Baltimore, Md.: Johns Hopkins University Press.

Murphy, Craig N. (1983). "What the Third World Wants: An Interpretation of the Development and Meaning of the New International Economic Order Ideology," *International Studies Quarterly*, vol. 27, no. 1 (March):55–76.

Myrdal, Gunnar. (1957). *Economic Theory and Underdeveloped Regions*. New York: Harper and Row.

Nanekar, S. R. (1973). "Public Administration Training for Change," *International Review of Administrative Sciences*, vol. 39, no. 1:56–60.

Ndongko, W. A., and S. O. Anyang. (1981). "The Concept of Appro-

120   REFERENCES

priate Technology: An Appraisal from the Third World,"
Monthly Review, vol. 32, no. 9 (February):35–43.

Noor, Abdun. (1981). *Education and Basic Human Needs*. Washington, D.C.: World Bank Staff Working Paper no. 450.

Nunes, F. E. (1974). "The Declining Status of the Jamaican Civil
Service," *Social and Economic Studies*, vol. 23, no. 2
(June):344–57.

Organisation for Economic Cooperation and Development. (1974).
Debt Problems of Developing Countries. Paris: OECD.

Oteiza, Enrique, and A. Rahman. (1978). "Technical Cooperation
among Third World Countries for Development," *Labour and
Society*, vol. 3, nos. 3–4 (July-October):445–56.

Packard, Phillip C. (1972). *Critical Path Analysis for Development
Administration*. The Hague: Mouton.

Palmer, Ransford W. (1979). *Caribbean Dependence on the United
States Economy*. New York: Praeger.

Parmar, Samuel L. (1975). "Self-Reliant Development in an 'Interdependent' World." In *Beyond Dependency: The Developing
World Speaks Out*. Ed. Guy F. Erb and Valeriana Kallab.
Washington, D.C.: Overseas Development Council.

Paul, Samuel. (1982). *Managing Development Programs: The Lessons of Success*. Boulder, Colo.: Westview Press.

———. (1983). *Strategic Management of Development Programmes*.
Geneva: ILO.

Peters, B. Guy. (1978). *The Politics of Bureaucracy*. New York:
Longman.

Quah, Jon S. T. (1976). "Administrative Reform: A Conceptual Analysis," *Philippine Journal of Public Administration*, vol. 20, no.
1 (January):50–67.

———. (1979). "Regressive Administration: Some Second Thoughts
on the Concept of Development Administration," *Administrative Change*, vol. 7, no. 1 (July-December):25–36.

Ramphal, Shridath S. (1978). "What Next? A Mandate for the Developing Countries." In *Partners in Tomorrow: Strategies for
a New International Order*. Ed. A. J. Dolman and J. van Ettinger. New York: E. P. Dutton.

Reubens, Edwin P. (1981). "An Overview of the NIEO." In *The
Challenge of the New International Economic Order*. Ed.
Edwin P. Reubens. Boulder, Colo.: Westview Press.

Riggs, Fred W. (1964). *Administration in Developing Countries: The
Theory of Prismatic Society*. Boston: Houghton Mifflin.

———. (1971). "The Context of Development Administration." In
Frontiers of Development Administration. Ed. Fred W. Riggs.
Durham, N.C.: Duke University Press.

Rondinelli, Dennis A. (1976). "Why Development Projects Fail: Some Problems of Project Management in Developing Countries," *Project Management Quarterly*, vol. 7, no. 1 (March):10–15.

————. (1981). "Government Decentralization in Comparative Perspective: Theory and Practice in Developing Countries," *International Review of Administrative Sciences*, vol. 47, no. 2:133–45.

Rothstein, Robert L. (1977). *The Weak in the World of the Strong.* New York: Columbia University Press.

St. Hill, C.A.P. (1970). "Towards Reform of the Public Services: Some Problems of Transitional Bureaucracies in Commonwealth Caribbean States," *Social and Economic Studies*, vol. 19, no. 1 (March):135–45.

Sauvant, Karl P. (1981). "The Origins of the NIEO Discussions." In *Changing Priorities on the International Agenda.* Ed. Karl P. Sauvant. New York: Pergamon Press.

Schumacher, E. F. (1974). *Small Is Beautiful: A Study of Economics As If People Mattered.* London: Abacus-Sphere Books.

Seers, Dudley. (1969). "The Meaning of Development," *International Development Review*, vol. 11, no. 4:2–6.

————. (1977). "The New Meaning of Development," *International Development Review*, vol. 19, no. 3:2–7.

Seidman, Harold. (1983). "Public Enterprise Autonomy: Need for a New Theory," *International Review of Administrative Sciences*, vol. 49, no. 1:65–72.

Sheahan, John B. (1976). "Public Enterprise in Developing Countries." In *Public Enterprise: Economic Analysis of Theory and Practice.* Ed. William G. Shepherd and Associates. Lexington, Mass.: D. C. Heath.

Singer, Hans. (1977). *Technologies for Basic Needs.* Geneva: ILO.

Singer, Hans, and J. A. Ansari. (1977). *Rich and Poor Countries.* Baltimore, Md.: Johns Hopkins University Press.

Srinivasan, T. N. (1977). "Development, Poverty, and Basic Human Needs: Some Issues," *Food Research Institute Studies*, vol. 16, no. 2:11–28.

Stone, Donald. (1966). "Guidelines for Training Development Administrators," *Journal of Administration Overseas*, vol. 5, no. 4 (October):229–42.

————. (1971). "Government Machinery Necessary for Development." In *Public Administration in Developing Countries.* Ed. Martin Kriesberg. Washington, D.C.: Brookings Institution.

————. (1973). "Removing Administrative and Planning Constraints to Development," *Journal of Administration Overseas*, vol. 12, no. 1 (January):4–10.

Stone, Donald, and Alice B. Stone. (1976). "Creation of Administrative Capability: The Missing Ingredient in Development Strategy." In *Strategy for Development*. Ed. John Barratt, David S. Collier, Kurt Glaser, and Herman Monnig. London: Macmillan Press.

Streeten, Paul. (1977). "The Distinctive Features of a Basic Needs Approach to Development," *International Development Review*, vol. 19, no. 3:8–16.

———. (1979a). "Basic Needs: Premises and Promises," *Journal of Policy Modeling*, vol. 1, no. 1:136–46.

———. (1979b). "Development Ideas in Historical Perspective." In *Toward a New Strategy for Development: A Rothko Chapel Colloqium*. Ed. K. Q. Hill. New York: Pergamon Press.

———. (1979c). "From Growth to Basic Needs," *Finance and Development*, vol. 16, no. 3 (September):28–31.

Streeten, Paul, and S. J. Burki. (1978). "Basic Needs: Some Issues," *World Development*, vol. 6, no. 3:411–21.

Swerdlow, Irving. (1975). *The Public Administration of Economic Development*. New York: Praeger.

———, ed. (1963). *Development Administration: Concepts and Problems*. Syracuse, N.Y.: Syracuse University Press.

Swerdlow, Irving, and Marcus Ingle, eds. (1974). *Public Administration Training for the Less Developed Countries*. Syracuse, N.Y.: Maxwell School of Citizenship and Public Affairs, Syracuse University.

Tait, Alan A.; Wilfred L. M. Grätz; and Barry J. Eichengreen. (1979). "International Comparisons of Taxation for Selected Developing Countries," *IMF Staff Papers*, vol. 26, no. 1 (March):123–56.

Tanzi, Vito. (1974). "The Theory of Tax Structure Development and the Design of Tax Structure Policy for Industrialisation." In *Fiscal Policy for Industrialisation in Latin America*. Ed. David Geithman. Gainesville: University of Florida Press.

Timsit, Gerard. (1981). "The Administrative Apparatus of States and the Implementation of the NIEO." In *Political and Institutional Issues of the NIEO*. Ed. E. Laszlo and J. Kurtzman. New York: Pergamon Press.

Tripathy, R. N. (1964). *Public Finance in Underdeveloped Countries*. Calcutta: World Press Private.

Tsurutani, T. (1973). *The Politics of National Development*. New York: Chandler Publishing Company.

United Nations. (1981). *Priority Areas for Action in Public Administration and Finance in the 1980s*. New York: U.N.

———. (1982). *Changes and Trends in Public Administration and Finance for Development: Second Survey 1977–1979.* New York: U.N.

Valenzuela, J. Samuel, and Arturo Valenzuela. (1981). "Modernisation and Dependency: Alternative Perspectives in the Study of Latin American Underdevelopment." In *From Dependency to Development: Strategies to Overcome Underdevelopment and Inequality.* Ed. Heraldo Munoz. Boulder, Colo.: Westview Press.

Waldo, Dwight, ed. (1970). *Temporal Dimensions of Development Administration.* Durham, N.C.: Duke University Press.

Watanabe, S. (1980). "Institutional Factors, Government Policies and Appropriate Technologies," *International Labour Review,* vol. 119, no. 2 (March-April):167–84.

Watson, Hilbourne. (1975). "Leadership and Imperialism in the Commonwealth Caribbean." In *The Commonwealth Caribbean into the Seventies.* Ed. A. W. Singham. Montreal: Centre for Developing Area Studies, McGill University.

Weidner, Edward W. (1962). "Development Administration: A New Focus of Research." In *Papers in Comparative Public Administration.* Ed. F. Heady and S. L. Stokes. Ann Arbor: Institute of Public Administration, University of Michigan.

Weiss, Moshe. (1966). "Some Suggestions for Improving Development Administration," *International Review of Administrative Sciences,* vol. 32, no. 3:193–96.

Wertheim, William F., and Matthias Stiefel. (1982). *Production, Equality and Participation in Rural China.* Geneva: UNRISD Participation Programme.

World Bank. (1980). *World Development Report, 1980.* Washington, D.C.: World Bank.

Wriggins, W. Howard, and Gunnar Adler-Karlsson. (1978). *Reducing Global Inequities.* New York: McGraw-Hill.

Zuvekas, Clarence. (1979). *Economic Development: An Introduction.* New York: St. Martin's Press.

Index

About the Author

KEMPE RONALD HOPE is Senior Fulbright Lecturer at the Institute of Social and Economic Research at the University of the West Indies in Kingston, Jamaica. He is the author of three other books: *Recent Performance and Trends in the Caribbean, Development Policy in Guyana,* and *The Post-War Planning Experience in Guyana.* He has published extensively in international journals including *World Development, Economica Internazionale,* and *Caribbean Geography.*